VISUAL
SHAKESPEARE

Essays in film and television

VISUAL SHAKESPEARE

Essays in film and television

GRAHAM HOLDERNESS

UNIVERSITY OF HERTFORDSHIRE PRESS

First published in Great Britain in 2002 by
University of Hertfordshire Press
Learning and Information Services
University of Hertfordshire
College Lane
Hatfield
Hertfordshire AL10 9AB

The right of Graham Holderness to be identified as author of this compilation has been asserted by him in accordance with the Copyright, Designs and Patents Act 1988.

Cover: Henry V (1984) © ITC/www.lfi.co.uk
Title page: The Chandos portrait attributed to John Taylor, c1610.
By courtesy of the National Portrait Gallery

A catalogue record for this book is available from the British Library.

ISBN 1 902806 13 1 paperback
ISBN 1 902806 16 6 casebound

Design by Geoff Green, Cambridge CB4 5RA
Cover design by John Robertshaw, Harpenden AL5 2JB
Printed in Great Britain by J. W. Arrowsmith Ltd, Bristol, BS3 2NT

For Christopher J. McCullough
vidimus oculis nostris

Contents

ॐ

Preface   ix

Television
1   Bard on the Box (1985, 1988)   3
2   Shakespeare Rescheduled (1998)   32

Film
3   Shakespeare and Cinema (1985, 1991)   51
4   Shakespeare Rewound (1993)   69

Case studies
5   Henry V (1984)   91
6   The Taming of the Shrew (1989)   124
7   Romeo and Juliet (1991)   151

Notes   183
Bibliography   197

Preface

༶

W HEN IN AN ESSAY published in *Shakespeare Survey* in 1987[1] Anthony Davies commented that "only comparatively recently has it become respectable to concentrate serious discussion on the media of cinema, radio and more especially television", the irony must to some extent have backfired. On the one hand one wanted to retort that exactly such 'serious attention' had been addressed to the 'mass media' by social scientists from the 1950s onwards. It was further apparent that the emergence and development of film, TV and media studies, which had followed hard upon the post-1968 renaissance in literary and cultural studies, had produced by 1987 some relatively mature and well-established disciplines. On the other hand Davies' point was correct insofar as it identified a substantial resistance to the new media from within the confines of Shakespeare studies.

This limitation to some extent derived from a general reluctance on the part of literary criticism to come to terms with radio, film and television. The very term 'mass media', with its associations of crude populism, commercial exploitation and the 'lowest common denominator' of culture, was readily adopted into literary criticism by, for example, Denys Thompson, and most influentially by F. R. Leavis, whose preoccupation with the civilising mission of high culture built an impermeable barrier against recognition of media production as culture at all in any but the anthropological sense.

At the same time, however, literary critics more open to studies in social science, philosophy and linguistics, and sharing a more radical political agenda (Richard Hoggart, Raymond Williams) began to open up spaces in the academy where serious study of the new media became possible. That Shakespeare studies still remained in 1987 relatively impervious to these changes is an indication of how parochial and intellectually dislocated 'the common pursuit of true judgement' had become.

This is particularly evident in the case of film, where the great acknowledged masterpieces of filmed Shakespeare – Olivier's *Henry V*, Kurosawa's *Macbeth* (*Throne of Blood*), Welles's *Othello*, Kozintsev's *Lear* – had between the end of the Second World War and 1970 established a formidable cinematic canon[2]. Yet as Davies's 1987 survey confirmed, only a handful of books had at that time been produced on Shakespeare and film.

The theatre has of course been recognised as the true home for Shakespearean production. This may seem self-evident given that the works in question are plays. But it is apparent from the critical history that printed Shakespeare was already something different from theatre, and attempts within certain critical formations (the Romantic movement, or the moment of Scrutiny) to detach Shakespeare's work from the theatre have been surprisingly successful. Nor has the relationship between academic study of Shakespeare and theatrical realisation always been an intimate one. In the eighteenth century theatre, Shakespeare was widely popular, but in the form of very free adaptations hardly recognisable to the scholars who were simultaneously seeking to stabilise the Shakespearean text. But since the theatre has become in the twentieth century a decidedly high cultural domain, the medium presents no impediment to the assimilation of a Shakespeare recognisable to literary criticism.

Cinema, however, was clearly different, as a relatively new technological medium that from the outset sought to build and maintain a popular audience. Anthony Davies described how deeply cinema was mistrusted by the academy, and more recently Robert Shaughnessy has noted that 'although a wide variety of cinematic versions, treatments, adaptations of, and borrowings from Shakespeare's plays have been part of the film industry's stock-in-trade from its earliest days … the belief that there may be a fundamental and irreconcilable antipathy between film (good or bad) and Shakespeare has persisted'[3]. This deep 'antipathy' explains what was until very recently a paucity of formal criticism in the field, and the lack of use made of Shakespeare on film as an educational resource. Both symptomatise a general perception that filmed Shakespeare was at best something of an irrelevance, and at worst a positively harmful influence on the study of Shakespeare as literature. Chapter One in this volume cites examples of 'O' level examiners' reports that clearly saw attention to filmed version of the plays as distractions from, or distortions of, the authentic Shakespearean text.

The problem was not just that literary criticism took an unconscionably long time to come to terms with film. When Shakespeare scholars eventually did begin to acknowledge film as a legitimate medium of Shakespearean production, what they found in film criticism was a discipline already transformed by the impact of critical theory, as described by Robert Shaughnessy:

> Classic film theory reproduces the central assumptions of the humanist critical tradition, in that aesthetic worth is measured in terms of its organic form, its thematic, stylistic and structural unity, its logic and coherence. Since 1968, however, the major currents in film theory have sought to challenge the assumptions of classic film criticism at the most fundamental level. (Shaughnessy, Shakespeare on Film, p. 6).

This generated a new set of problems for practitioners who were seeking an accommodation between Shakespeare and film but who remained still attached to traditional literary critical methods and principles. 'What was new', wrote Robert Lapsley and Michael Westlake, 'was the fact that theory no longer sought accommodation with the existing criticism and aesthetics, and was not presented as an improvement or refinement of current critical practice, but was avowedly bent on its overthrow'.[4] For those still working within the 'humanist critical tradition' this transformation was problematic since it was difficult to align the values of the critical tradition with the logic of the film medium. As Shaughnessy puts it, 'if traditional film critics prized organic unity as a central principle, more recent criticism has found that the interest of a film text lies in its contradictions and self-divisions, its gaps, silences and evasions' (Shaughnessy, *Shakespeare on Film*, p. 8).

The essays in this volume, published from 1984 onwards, drew their theoretical parameters from post-1968 film theory and from the theoretically influenced literary criticism of the same period. The two essays on television Shakespeare, with which the volume begins, centre naturally on the output of the BBC, reading Shakespeare productions in the light of the producing institution's general character, but also examine productions from other television networks by way of cultural comparison. The discussions of film focus variously on: the relationship between the Shakespeare text and the cinematic version (especially Chapter Four); a play's theatre history and its transmutation to film (Chapter Seven); the influences of theatre and film industry on Shakespearean film production (Chapter Six); the socio-historical and cultural-political contexts impinging on a film's making (Chapter Five). The two general essays with which the volume begins draw all these contexts into focus and explain why the processes of film and television adaptation are here seen more as acts of translation than of realisation. Filmed or televised versions of Shakespeare's plays are productions, not in the passive sense (a 'performance' of something else, the play) but in the active sense that film produces an entirely new and different Shakespeare from the Shakespeare of the literary text or the Shakespeare of the theatre.

Today the academic scene is very different from what it was in

1987. There are many more Shakespeare films and many more books on them; and filmed Shakespeare has become a normal and legitimate part of Shakespeare studies. Critics now routinely acknowledge and address films which would once not have been recognised as 'filmed Shakespeare' at all – modern appropriations such as Baz Luhrmann's *Romeo and Juliet*, or films that adapt Shakespearean language, plots and situations to a contemporary theme, such as Gus van Sant's *My Private Idaho*. Shakespeare films are also now used much more extensively in the teaching of Shakespeare, confirming the emphasis I placed on this dimension in the 1985 essay that now forms Chapter Three of this volume.[5] I hope the reader will find in these pages some examples of work that helped to enable that distinct cultural transformation.

PART ONE

Television

CHAPTER ONE

Bard on the Box (1985, 1988)

Elizabeth by the grace of God Queen of England, etc., to all Justices, Mayors, Sherriffs, Bailliffs, Head Constables, Under Constables, and all other our officers and ministers, greeting. Know ye that we of our especial grace, certain knowledge and mere motion have licensed and authorised, and by these presents do licence and authorise, our loving subjects, James Burbage, John Perkin, John Lanham, William Johnson, and Robert Wilson, servants to our trusty and well-beloved Cousin and Counsellor the Earl of Leicester, to use, exercise and occupy the art and faculty of playing Comedies, Tragedies, interludes, stage plays ... [1]

Elizabeth by the Grace of God of the United Kingdom of Great Britain and Northern Ireland and of our other Realms and Territories Queen, Head of the Commonwealth, Defender of the Faith:
TO ALL TO WHOM THESE PRESENTS SHALL COME, GREETINGS! ...
NOW KNOW YE that We, by our Prerogative Royal and of Our especial grace, certain knowledge and mere motion do this by Our Charter for Us, Our Heirs and Successors will, ordaine and declare as follows ... [2]

THE SECOND QUOTATION is not an address from the first Elizabeth to her loving subjects, or (as the first quotation is) a licence granting liberty to a sixteenth-century acting company. It is a proclamation, dated 1981, of Elizabeth, the second of that name, formally granting a Royal Charter to the British Broadcasting Corporation.

WHEREAS in view of the widespread interest which is taken by
Our Peoples in broadcasting services and of the great value of
such services as a means of disseminating information, education and entertainment, We believe it to be in the interests of Our
Peoples in Our United Kingdom and elsewhere within the Commonwealth that the Corporation should continue to provide
broadcasting services pursuant to such licences and agreements in
that behalf as Our Secretary of State may from time to time grant
and make with the Corporation.

This formal act of authorisation, issued by the highest levels of
the state, draws on the linguistic, cultural and political heritage of
the first Elizabethan Age. In return for the powers thus clothed in
ornate language and rich cultural currency, the Corporation has
consistently, and more than any other broadcasting institution or
medium, preserved in active and perpetuated forms the most
striking and singular product of that earlier age, the cultural
phenomenon we know as 'Shakespeare'.

ৡ

Although it could be argued that the founding fathers of the BBC
chose incorporation by Royal Charter rather than Parliamentary
Statute in order to secure political independence rather than
antique dignity, the parallel with the Elizabethan theatre is
irresistible. In the space of some thirty years, at the end of the
sixteenth century a varied, heterogeneous and pluralistic medium
became a virtual (and after the Restoration an actual) state
monopoly.[3] When the BBC was granted its first Royal Charter in
1927 and 'public service broadcasting' was born, a relatively new
technological medium with enormous and hugely varied possibilities (some of which are only now about to penetrate British
society) was shaped into a national institution. The BBC
emerged, like the Elizabethan theatre, in a post-war cultural crisis
in which there was a pressing need for the development of a new
sense of national identity:

The very condition for its existence coincided with the need for a new definition of the nation ... In the wake of the scramble for colonies, the first imperialist war, the growth of American capital and the partition of Ireland, it was evident that 'Britishness' was not simply something present and permanent, it was something to be produced in a continual process of cultural reformation. The BBC does not reflect or represent an already fully formed national consciousness, a coherent national identity, rather it is one of several material agents or 'national' institutions which produce and reproduce that very identity.[4]

The guiding intelligence and moral zeal behind the construction of the BBC as a kind of national church were those of John Reith, who was appointed as the Corporation's general manager, later its Director-General, and subsequently elevated to the peerage for his services to the establishment. Reith's Memorandum to the Crawford Committee, set up in 1925 to prepare plans for the new broadcasting monopoly, represents a concise statement of principles which still lie at the root of the theory of public service broadcasting. Echoing his Arnoldian inheritance, Reith articulated his vision of the new medium penetrating not only the cultural but the moral, intellectual and spiritual life of the nation: 'the Broadcasting Service should bring into the greatest possible number of homes in the fullest degree all that is best in every department of human knowledge, endeavour and achievement – the Service must not be used for entertainment purposes alone'. The Reithian Sunday was the most intense focus of his evangelical fervour for moral improvement: 'the programmes which are broadcast on Sunday are therefore framed with the day itself in mind ... I believe that Sabbaths should be one of the most valuable assets of our existence – quiet islands on the tossing sea of life'.[5] There were to be no transmissions during hours of worship except where the transmission was of a complete church service. The BBC tradition of promoting edifying material on Sundays persists to this day: the BBC/Time-Life Shakespeare productions were all broadcast, perhaps in memory of Lord Reith, on Sunday evenings.

Regarded as an institution, the BBC has often seemed little more than an agency, if not a department, of government. Established as a supposedly independent body, in its early years it operated aggressively to identify the interests of the state and the interests of the people. In the General Strike of 1926 the Corporation acted as an instrument of centralised propaganda. 'There could be no question about our supporting the government in general' said Reith, 'since the BBC was a national institution and since the Government in this crisis was acting for the people … the BBC was for the Government in the crisis too'.[6] The identification of Government and people was clearly a strategy of ideological conciliation; the identification of the BBC with the people a ludicrously inappropriate populist gesture: 'Whatever its aspirations at the time, the BBC could hardly be said to be speaking for Britain, still less *to* it. Its relative newness, its self-denying ordinance against dealing with "controversial" matters, all mitigated against a true involvement with the deeper and more varied levels of the society'.[7]

> In fact as an institution the primary ideological function of the BBC remains that of constructing a coherent version of a unified nation calculated to elide political, economic and cultural realities: 'The BBC is a national institution in so far as it consistently promotes the illusion of a unified and integrated political region with a system of common values and beliefs. Its very existence perpetuates this myth'. (Maley, 'Centralisation', p. 37)

Television, as Marshall McLuhan observed, is an inherently *social* medium; it invites group rather than individual participation. It is easy to mistake the particular forms in which a medium is commercially and politically exploited for the character of the form itself: there is no necessary relationship between the medium of television and the dissemination of small receivers for use within individual homes. When we see a group of people watching a sporting event on television in a pub, we see the medium making for lively social interchange rather than isolated individual absorption. As it is, television operates as a medium of collective participation within that fundamental social institution the family (however constituted) and within that basic space of social living, the home. Secondly, television is a universal medium to a far greater extent than the theatre or even literacy: as an oral and visual form it is accessible even to the unlettered, its complex visual dialect easier to learn than spoken or written language. It can therefore claim, more than any other cultural form, to be a national communications medium, the primary system of an authentically 'national' culture. More so than print (even popular newspapers) certainly more so than other 'cultural' discourses such as literature and theatre, television has succeeded in incorporating itself into the rhythms of social life, so that the medium has become a normal part of everyday experience. The act of reading involves isolation, physical separation, withdrawal: while attendance at a concert or art gallery, a visit to a theatre or cinema, involve abandonment of ordinary patterns of behaviour, the allocation of a 'special' occasion in a cultural space separate from the concrete texture of everyday living. Television, requiring no such privileged deviation from social activity, can be regarded as a peculiarly general and populist cultural form.

Such characteristics of the medium have led some writers to draw comparisons between television *as a medium* and the Elizabethan popular drama. Terry Hawkes in *Shakespeare's Talking Animals* proposed the television medium as a successor to, or reconstitution of, the cultural potentialities of the Elizabethan playhouse. Both television and the Elizabethan theatre offer *communal* rather than solitary experiences, permitting active and simultaneous discussion and response. The modern theatre is no longer a communal but a minority art, where television is both populist and democratic. Both television and the Elizabethan drama can be described, within their respective cultures, as 'natural' activities, not distinct from the common flow of everyday living. The 'whole experience' of cinema or theatre – surrounded and interrupted, certainly, by moments of social intercourse such as intervals – involve isolation in the darkness and imposed silence of an auditorium: the brightly – lit screen or picture-frame stage commands a hypnotised absorption into an aesthetic totality. Television interacts with known and familiar surroundings so that the complex unity of its characteristic experience has a quality of multifariousness absent from all cinema and most theatre.

Such parallels between the television medium and the Elizabethan drama have certainly been expressed consistently by those involved in producing Shakespeare for the BBC. In 1947 George More O'Ferrall wrote of his production of *Hamlet*: 'Why should we claim that television is especially suited to Shakespeare? Because in its method of presentation it comes nearer to the Elizabethan theatre, for which the plays were written, than the modern theatre can do'.[8] The parallel characteristics cited are diversified acting areas, swift sequence of scenes and the possibility of intimacy between actor and audience. John Wilders, Literary Consultant to the BBC/Time-Life Shakespeare series, pursued this analogy to claim that television reproduction of Shakespeare could emulate or at least approach the freedom and flexibility of Renaissance popular drama.[9]

Raymond Williams has shown[10] that in all developed broadcasting systems the characteristic organisation is one of 'sequence' or 'flow'. In all communications systems before broadcasting, the essential items were discrete, independent units: in broadcasting the real *programme* is offered as a sequence of these and other similar events, which are then available in a single dimension and a single operation.

Broadcasting in its early stages inherited this problematic, and – since in general the form of the technology developed prior to any corresponding content – operated in a parasitic way upon it. The philosophy of broadcasting was 'transmission', the relaying of events (musical concert, play, public address, sporting event) to a general audience. Programming was a matter of arranging these discrete televised events into a series of timed units, with the appropriate mix, balance and proportion.

In Williams's view the important change was the movement, inherent in the nature of the medium itself, towards a concept of sequence not as programming but as a continuous *flow*. This is recognised instinctively in the way we talk of 'watching television' rather than watching a particular unit, and in the familiar reluctance to 'switch off' after a unit is completed. What the viewer experiences is thus not the published programme of discrete units but a planned flow which is in both form and content the real 'broadcasting'.

ఠ

BBC television began to dramatise productions of Shakespeare from its inception, the first occurring in February 1937. There was already a strong tradition of broadcasting Renaissance drama in general on BBC *radio*[11] but BBC television, with some exceptions, has never followed this, choosing always to paddle in the safer shallows of Shakespeare.

The challenge of adapting Shakespeare for television was certainly taken up at an early stage but a close attention to the particular forms employed can be instructive. The first complete production (of *Julius Caesar*) was broadcast in July 1938: prior to this there had been some twenty broadcasts in the form of a series called 'Scenes from Shakespeare'. The programmes would be about twenty-five minutes in duration, comparable with other types of programme. Programming information foregrounded the *actors* rather than the play or the dramatist, in keeping with a similar emphasis for light entertainment programmes, music, comedy and so forth. Caution should be exercised in drawing inferences from this form, since before the war television broadcasting was in a very early experimental stage and the technologies relatively undeveloped. Notwithstanding, it can be suggested that initially television incorporated and assimilated Shakespeare into, and employed methods of production and transmission appropriate to, its own medium. Despite the strong and evident influence of the theatrical profession (at its strongest in the 1950s) television did not seek to come to terms with Shakespeare on grounds defined by the theatre or literary criticism. Whole plays were broken into 'scenes from', short units compatible with normal programming requirements. Duration of programme units was not in itself a technical inhibition: in March 1937 a relatively full fifty-minute version of *Macbeth* (longer than many a supposedly complete silent production) was broadcast in two halves. The format was the result of programming decisions: Shakespeare was programmed as 'entertainment' rather than as 'education' or 'information'. The emphasis on the distinctive qualities of actors, derived directly from the contemporary theatre, paralleled the star cult of 'variety' common in both the contemporary cinema and in television itself.

Initially, television approached Shakespeare in a manner very different from the broadcasting techniques we have become accustomed to. The material was treated as entertainment; incorporated into a pattern of mixed programming without any unusual emphasis or special foregrounding and regarded as not essentially different from any other item placed within a particular programmed sequence. Nor is there any manifestation, in these early stages, of the ideological appropriation of Shakespeare which later became commonplace. On St George's Day in 1936 there was no broadcast of *Henry V*: instead there was a documentary about another national culture hero, King Arthur. The *Radio Times* of 1937 carried an enormous amount of media 'hype' around the coronation of George VI: even by the standards of contemporary media servility towards royalty, the number of programming references and exploitations of popular monarchist interest is extraordinary. There were programmes on heraldry, royal families and even archery appropriated as 'toxophily – the sport of kings'. There were advertisements using the occasion for commercial opportunism. There was a broadcast performance of Edward German's *Merrie England*. But there was no Shakespeare.

Even BBC Radio offered only a paltry twenty minutes of *Henry V*, compared with the whole of Act 3 of Wagner's *Die Walküre*, and to supply a more patriotic air, 'the song of a nightingale, broadcast from a wood in Surrey'.[12]

After the war BBC television moved into Shakespeare production in a much more confident way, and by the early 1950s the modern format of BBC Shakespeare, monumentally established in the BBC/Time-Life Series, was more or less fully formed. Where the early broadcast performances integrated the productions into the programmed sequence of variety and entertainment, adapting the material to the rhythms of the medium: from the early 1950s the Corporation began to make Shakespeare broadcasts into special occasions by programming on particular seasonal dates – *Twelfth Night* at Christmas, *Henry V* on St George's Day; by using a particularly significant 'slot' such as Sunday evening and by inserting write-ups and feature articles into the *Radio Times* to prepare the viewer for an isolated, special experience. In the late 1940s plays were broadcast in complete versions from studios and by outside broadcast.[13] The first production of *Hamlet* in December 1947 sprawled magisterially across four evenings.[14] The *Radio Times* carried a feature article by the producer, which claimed in his support the theatrical and academic authority of Dover Wilson and Granville Barker. The production was highlighted in the 'recommended viewing' column, 'Talk of the Week'. *Hamlet* was followed in 1949-50 by the other three 'great tragedies', each accompanied by supportive feature articles in the *Radio Times*.[15]

By the early 1950s everything possible was being done to isolate a Shakespeare performance from the flow or sequence of the medium. A special kind of privileged attention was being focused on the play by accompanying 'programme notes' and quasi-academic discussions. The practice of flanking a performance with educative ancillary material was beginning to appear: on the evening of 'Shakespeare's Birthday' (23 April) 1952, to herald a production of *The Taming of the Shrew*, a panel discussion on 'Televising Shakespeare' featured producers, actors and critics.[16] In the *Radio Times* a visual technique of boxing information on the play, to separate it from the contamination of the surrounding contextual *bricolage*, began to be employed. A useful example of the latter is to be found in the *Radio Times* for 15 May 1953. The programme note on the play, a production of *Henry V*, is boxed off from the surrounding page in a design resembling a theatrical programme. A short article by Michael Macowan, the BBC producer, is incorporated into the programming information, describing the acting company and its methods. The company in question was called the 'Elizabethan Theatre Company':

> With very little money, and using the barest minimum of setting and the most elementary Elizabethan costumes, a dozen to a score of young men and women, mostly from Oxford and Cambridge, set out last summer to play Shakespeare wherever they could find an audience and a place to play in. Sometimes it was an inn yard, sometimes a college garden or the hall of an ancient house (the kind of conditions which Shakespeare's own company met on their tours), sometimes a town hall or an ordinary theatre.[17]

This touring company, based on the principle of reviving the Elizabethan *ensemble* – playing in extra-theatrical locations, without pictorial scenery, doubling parts – was a characteristic product of what Alan Sinfield has called 'culturalism'. A product of the relative cultural fertility of post-war Britain, this intervention attempted to offer an alternative to mainstream theatrical tradition, aligning Shakespeare more closely with notions of accessible popular entertainment. The production was directed by John Barton and subsidised by (among others) the Arts Council.

The Elizabethan Theatre Company was also a forerunner of the early RSC and, without making extravagant claims for the radical potentiality of this embryo which is now a monumental national institution, it can be suggested that the kind of dramatic intervention made here was culturally a potential point of radical energy in Shakespeare reproduction; and its presentation on television a challenge to the dominant theatrical and naturalistic conventions. Yet this remarkable production of *Henry V* appeared as the BBC's official contribution to the festivities for the coronation of Elizabeth II. The *Radio Times*' 'Television Diary' juxtaposed 'The Elizabethan Theatre Company' against a BBC film on 'The Second Elizabeth'. A potential growth-point of post-war British culture, which was attempting by a reappropriation of Elizabethan theatrical practices to harness some of the popular energies of the Renaissance theatre, was in turn appropriated by the BBC and manipulated into a curtain-raiser for the New Elizabethan Age. An opportunity of bringing the populist and democratic medium of television into an alliance with the popular aspects of Shakespearean theatre was rendered by the operation of institutional forces little more than an ideological affirmation of historical continuity, institutional hegemony and State power.

ॐ

'Television constitutes the only really "national" theatre our society is likely to have.'[18] The medium of television would appear to offer unique opportunities for a democratic recovery of Shakespeare: a reappropriation of jealously guarded fortresses of high culture for the popular audience which initially embraced and fostered the Elizabethan drama. As we have seen, television is (unlike the Elizabethan theatre) a national institution in a genuinely universal sense; its place that fundamental space of social life, the home; its mode of communication direct, populist and general; its content largely constituted by the 'entertainment' and information widely regarded as the staple necessities of our contemporary culture. The close parallel drawn by Terry Hawkes was echoed by John Wilders, literary adviser to the BBC Shakespeare series, who followed the analogy to propose

that TV reproduction of Shakespeare's drama can emulate, or at
least approach, the freedom and flexibility of Shakespeare's contemporary stage.[19] Thus that cultural comparison with which we
began, between the BBC and the Elizabethan theatre, appears to
underlie the largest ever investment of television in Shakespeare,
the BBC/Time-Life Shakespeare series.

Whether in practice television adaptations of Shakespeare
genuinely fulfil these ambitions – and, indeed, whether the
Elizabethan theatre can be properly regarded in retrospect as the
central focus of national culture – are affirmations that remain
open to question. A different kind of populism emerges from
within the BBC itself: where academics envisage television as a
means of reconstituting the Elizabethan theatre, producers think
more in terms of translating theatre into the familiar discourse of
television itself. For Cedric Messina, the original producer
(replaced after the first two years by Jonathan Miller) the 'primary purpose of the series' was 'to provide good entertainment
… because that's what Shakespeare wrote them for'.[20] 'The guiding principle … is to make the plays, in permanent form, accessible to audiences throughout the world.'[21] Within this alliance
of academics and broadcasters there naturally arose a certain
tension, between, on the one hand, scholarly and educational
concerns and on the other, the values of popular entertainment;
with the TV medium usually imposing its own solution, as John
Wilders indicates: 'The television equivalent of Shakespeare's
stage would be an empty studio … I am now certain however
that we were right not to adopt this style … to the television
viewer, accustomed as he is to such representations of reality as
football matches, news films, and thrillers filmed on location in
California, the opening scene of *Macbeth* would not have been
"an open place" but Studio 1 of the Television Centre, White City'
(Wilders, 'Adjusting the set', p.13). None the less, within that
alliance of the camera and the pen, these discrete ideologies, the
scholarly/democratic and the media-populist, seem to have
coalesced into unity: and the tendency of the resultant approach

to Shakespeare must necessarily move towards a devolution of cultural power, an undermining of 'Shakespeare' as a symbol of cultural authority.

The argument for 'accessibility' is greatly strengthened by the (now familiar but actually very recent) developments in the manufacture and marketing of video technology. Broadcasting itself makes the complex and expensive products of an intensely centralised culture immediately available to the whole of a society but the availability remains at the mercy of centralised planning bodies and not at all subject to popular participation or democratic control. Video technology increases the availability enormously and (however severely constrained by restrictive copyright legislation and the absence of a licensing system) confers much more power on the consumer. The planners of the BBC Shakespeare had this in mind from the outset: Cedric Messina accepted the suggestion that one hope of the planners was for the creation of 'a library of Shakespeare video productions that will last for quite some time'. This aspiration involved commercial as well as cultural considerations: ' … the plays are actually starting to pay for themselves. The plays are selling already around the world … ' ('Cedric Messina discusses *The Shakespeare Plays*', p.135).

In one sense, and particularly for those operating within the educational apparatus of 'Literature', the translation of Shakespeare into a non-literary form must necessarily be *potentially* radical: subverting the cultural hegemony of literature itself, disturbing the equilibrium of received cultural traditions. Similarly, if one symptomatic strategy of bourgeois culture is to preserve certain figures of cultural authority for specialised participation by a social and intellectual élite, then the extension of participation in Shakespeare to a much wider constituency *via* that audience's most familiar medium, must necessarily exert some pressure on the bases of cultural power. But these propositions bring us up against the truly fundamental question: is the extension of high culture to be seen as a democratic appropriation of cultural wealth by the people; or simply as an extension of centralised cultural power by the transmission of authority, in the form of an art which *cannot choose but* be reactionary and pacificatory in its ideological effects? After all, Matthew Arnold, and the *Newbolt Report*, and *Scrutiny*, all spoke of the desirability of taking Shakespeare to the masses, often in a rhetoric of intense radical populism: but they were certainly not fostering or proposing a radical cultural politics.

Although, as previously demonstrated, productions of Shakespeare on TV are nothing new, the project of the series, in its ambitious scope and scale and massive investment of cultural capital, clearly represents the most significant intervention to date into the reproduction of Shakespeare on the screen. And other, more material investment was required to get the series off the ground: the BBC entered into partnership with the American company Time-Life TV, which in turn raised financial backing for the series from three big private corporations in the USA – Exxon Corporation, Metropolitan Life Insurance Company and Morgan Guaranty Trust Company of New York. This alliance between the BBC and American private enterprise indicates how the series was generated from the very highest levels of economic and cultural power. Clearly it is inadequate to write off the series as a predictable symptom of its institutional and capitalistic origin but it is important to trace and measure the constraints and determinants built into the series itself as a consequence of its economic and institutional basis.

The scale of investment and the nature of commercial under-writing (as distinct from commercial *sponsorship*) imposed one very obvious requirement on this enterprise: it should be economically viable; that is, give an economic as well as a cultural return on capital investment. This condition necessarily entailed the preservation of the plays in a consumer-durable form (video-cassette) rather than restriction to one-off transmission, and an international marketing operation. Conscious of this dependence on the market rather than on patronage and subsidy, the planners insisted that productions should aim for 'high quality' and 'durability'. What 'high quality' originally implied in such a context is predicable: 'great' directors, 'classical' actors, 'straightforward' productions: ' ... these productions will offer a wonderful opportunity to study the plays performed by some of the greatest classical actors of our time' (Messina, 'Preface' to *Richard II*, p. 8). This insistence on building into the productions that isolating quality of 'excellence' is familiar from the Arnoldian practices of literary criticism: though it is perhaps unusual to find critical excellence and market value, the common pursuit of true judgement and industrial quality control, quite so firmly identified. The concept of 'high quality' in fact entailed a conservative respect for 'traditional' values in Shakespearean production. Jonathan Miller has described the 'problems' he inherited in taking over the series, among them '... the original contract with the American co-producers – it had to be so-called traditional ...'.[22] Cedric Messina had accepted this constraint even more readily, in the belief that only 'traditional' productions would 'stand the test of time': 'We've not done anything too sensational in the shooting of it – there's no arty-crafty shooting at all. All of them are, for want of a better word, straightforward productions' ('Cedric Messina discusses *The Shakespeare Plays*', p.137).

Despite expressed reservations, Jonathan Miller accepted the executive producership of the series after the second season. Whatever his capacities as a stage director, Miller believes in the absolute determinacy of the television medium, which imposes its own constraints on dramatic production. Television is incurably naturalistic and translates everything into naturalism.[23] Miller is therefore averse to any attempt to theatricalise television: TV productions should display no manneristic theatrical styles, no expressionistic acting and no mixing of conventions. It is impossible to reproduce Elizabethan theatre conditions in a television presentation: 'What is characteristic about the Elizabethan stage condition is that the audience is part of that condition ... In television you automatically eliminate the audience. It isn't present at the production. It's absolutely hopeless to try and reconstitute the wooden "O" inside the electronic square' (Slater, 'An interview with Jonathan Miller', p. 9). Olivier's film version of *Henry V* was therefore mistaken in trying 'to set up within one medium the conventions of another'. Miller's constant adherence to naturalism is admitted as an explicit commitment to illusionist representation: the audience should be 'unaware of the fact that they're in the presence of an art-form'.

In fact there is greater diversity of production styles in the series than these theoretical pronouncements would suggest. But there can be little doubt that overall a conservative 'drag' is applied by a combination of factors: the constraints of commercial underwriting; the consequent concern of the BBC to build high quality prestige into the series; the conservative cultural views of the original producer and the willing submission of his successor to the dominant naturalistic style of television drama. The conservatism of the whole series can best be measured against one remarkable exception – Jane Howell's production of the first historical tetralogy.

The most appropriate contrast of detail to be made is that between the productions of the second historical tetralogy (which belongs to the first and second 'seasons' of 1978–9), directed by David Giles under the producership of Cedric Messina, and the 1982 productions of *Henry VI* and *Richard III*. Messina foregrounded the English history cycle, allowing these plays to dominate the first two seasons (*Richard II* and *Henry VIII* in 1978; the *Henry IV*s and *Henry V* in 1979). These programming decisions suggest a nationalistic desire to celebrate the course of English history, but the 'British' quality emerges also from Messina's thoroughly conventional view of the plays: 'These histories are a sort of curse of the House of Atreus in English'. This view was supported by an ancillary broadcast featuring right-wing pundit Paul Johnson: 'According to the orthodox Tudor view of history the deposition of the rightful and anointed king,

Richard II, was a crime against God, which thereafter had to be expiated by the nation in a series of bloody struggles ... '.[24] Messina wanted to organise the plays into a coherent historical totality. It was originally the producer's hope that the plays would share a uniformity of style, knitting them even more closely together into an integrated unity. Asked by an interviewer what he would be doing to 'assure continuity', Messina spoke of maintaining character castings and indicated that he thought it would be 'right and proper' to keep the same director ('Cedric Messina discusses The Shakespeare Plays', p. 137).

This didn't, in the event, happen: and the consequences are instructive. The second tetralogy is a characteristic example of conventional 'high quality' Shakespearean production: performed, in Messina's words 'by a splendid company, including many of the leading names in our classical drama' (Messina, 'Preface' to Richard II, p. 9). The central actors tend to be classical old stagers or modern stars: John Geilgud, Wendy Hiller, Anthony Quayle, Derek Jacobi and Jon Finch. The overall style of production is overwhelmingly naturalistic; the director David Giles was chosen as an experienced television director regarded as 'adept at dealing with English history and the English character' (e.g. The Forsyte Saga) (ibid., p. 19). The combat scene in Richard II (I.iii), a formalised heraldic ritual which hardly invites naturalistic presentation, was done in this mode: 'You can't do it realistically in a television studio and yet we didn't want it to get too stylised: that's why we used real horses. If we had gone too stylised with the list scene we would have had to stylise the play all the way through, and stylisation on television is very difficult' (David Giles in BBC Richard II, p. 20).

The second tetralogy emerges from this production as a constituent element in an inclusive and integrated dramatic totality, illustrating the violation of natural social 'order' by the deposition of a legitimate king. The plays are produced in 'classic drama' style with predominantly naturalistic devices of acting, mise-en-scène and filming. Actors are identified wholly with their roles, growing old in them; settings are more naturalistic than conventionalised; camera movements and angles are always 'straightforward', with no 'arty-crafty' shooting.

In the case of Jane Howell's productions of the first historical tetralogy, the director's whole conception of the Shakespearean history play diverges strikingly from that propounded by Cedric Messina and evidently accepted by David Giles. Where Messina saw the history plays conventionally as orthodox Tudor historiography, and the director employed dramatic techniques which allow that ideology a free and unhampered passage to the spectator, Jane Howell took a more complex view of the first tetralogy as, simultaneously, a serious attempt at historical interpretation, and as a drama with a peculiarly modern relevance and contemporary application. The plays, to this director, were not a dramatisation of the Elizabethan World Picture but a sustained interrogation of residual and emergent ideologies in a changing society.[25] Commenting on Talbot's dilemma in *I Henry VI*, IV.v–vi, Howell defines the drama as a disclosure of the contradictoriness of chivalric values: 'When Talbot finally comes face to face with his own son who will not leave the battle although he knows he is going to get killed, then Talbot has to come face to face with his own values; because if the values of chivalry mean you have to sacrifice your son … ' (*BBC I Henry VI*, p. 31). At the same time Howell wanted to explore the plays' potentiality for contemporary signification: 'We felt it shouldn't be too mediaeval … we talked about Northern Ireland and Beirut and South America, about warlords and factions'.[26] This awareness of the multiplicity of potential meanings in the play required a decisive and scrupulous avoidance of television or theatrical naturalism: methods of production should operate to open the plays out, rather than close them into the immediately recognisable familiarity of conventional Shakespearean production.

Howell's basic conception of the plays entailed a refusal to attempt naturalism: Jonathan Miller's insistence that the TV medium *enforces* naturalism, and that the conventions of theatre would not work within it, seems to have been systematically ignored: 'At the outset she had made the clear decision to avoid any attempt to scale down the action to make it more "televisual". The energy, she felt, was essentially theatrical and she therefore made a number of theatrical decisions – the company would double parts as they do in the theatre; the action would all take place on a single set, which would change in mood from play to play ... ' (Fenwick, 'Dialogues of Disintegration', p. 20). One important consideration here was a historical one: Howell felt that the plays would work better in the kind of theatrical situation they were originally produced in, on a relatively bare stage with minimal, emblematic props and scenery, by a company of actors operating as an *ensemble*. The set, modelled on an adventure playground in Fulham, was designed to suggest the locations of popular drama – 'we thought of fairgrounds and circuses and mystery plays' as well as familiar modern environments, a children's playground or a burnt-out building site. It was constructed to appear deliberately non-naturalistic: thus allowing the play to express both historical and contemporary meanings. Oliver Bayldon, the set designer, explained his decision to use a modern parquet floor as a deliberate violation of illusionist representation: 'It stops the set from literally representing ... it reminds us we are in a modern television studio'.[27] Stanley Wells commended this aspect of the production: 'Jane Howell has dared to encourage us to remember that the action is taking place in a studio'.[28]

It will be apparent to what extent Jane Howell's practice contradicts or negates the definitive pronouncements of Cedric Messina and Jonathan Miller on how Shakespeare should be televised. This director found it possible to reject television naturalism in favour of the theatricalising of television; to mix the conventions of one medium with those of another; and to recreate some of the radical potentialities of the Elizabethan theatre. Even Jonathan Miller's persuasive point about TV's elimination of the audience was solved here by constituting members of the cast, for certain scenes, as a vociferous and participating audience (e.g. the Jack Cade scenes in *2 Henry VI*); as well as by extensive use of the direct address to camera, the equivalent of actor-audience dialogue.

All these devices are defamiliarising, estranging, 'alienating'; they induce the kind of alert and vigilant curiosity sought by Brecht's 'epic' theatre. The actors double parts, thus preventing an illusionary identification of actor and character. Nor are the actors the familiar Shakespearean stars of the BBC *Richard II*, whose personalities seem so 'subdued so what they work in' that they appear to *be* characters from Shakespeare. Furthermore, under the director's influence there is a general rejection of Stanislavskian method: her advice to her actors insistently recalls Brecht (see *BBC 2 Henry VI*, p. 24). This 'epic' style provides much greater flexibility and freedom to the actor, who is no longer imprisoned within the naturalist concept of a coherent psychological identity, but able to play out those psychological incoherences which can disclose sociological truths (see *BBC I Henry VI*, p. 30).

♨

The radical potentialities of television Shakespeare, evident enough from these examples, are in practice systematically blocked, suppressed or marginalised by the conservatism of the dominant cultural institutions. Overall the BBC Shakespeare series operates to confirm the cultural authority which in turn confers the status of high culture upon the BBC itself, and on those powerful capitalist corporations which financed it – a circular process which effectively closes out the people for whom the series is supposedly produced. Once the production becomes completed and packaged in video-cassette form it becomes universally available, but also permanently fixed, unchangeable: the radical and subversive potentiality of performance is translated back into something closer to the authoritarian dominance of the literary text. The BBC Shakespeare series is in fact the most perfect consummation to date of a process which commenced in Shakespeare's own time, with the Tudor government's systematic destruction of the national religious drama, the professionalising of theatre by the licensing of a few acting companies and the building of the first purpose-built playhouses; the privileging of metropolitan over national culture, and the incorporation of the drama into the cultural structure of an emergent bourgeois nation-State. A 'national' culture is, in bourgeois terms, the production by a centralised cultural apparatus, operating from the capital, of high-quality aesthetic objects which are then transmitted to the 'nation', which in turn acts as passive recipient of a pre-packaged cultural commodity. The active, democratic participation and intervention of the Elizabethan audience actually generated a process which reduced that audience to an inert constituency loyally consuming liberal doses of what one is tempted to call, following Peter Brook, 'deadly television'.[29]

The BBC/Time-Life Shakespeare series was produced in the image of the Corporation itself, as a classical monument of national culture, or an oppressive agency of cultural hegemony. The nature of the product itself inevitably acts to solidify the conservative tendencies of the institution, and to inhibit resistance from within. Hence the possibilities for alternative or oppositional reproduction of Shakespeare must be sought more generally outside the BBC. Channel Four, in keeping with its generally radical-liberal approach to cultural matters, succeeded in providing an impressive piece of marginal opposition in the series *Shakespeare Lives!* (broadcast January–March 1983). Director Michael Bogdanov assembled a group of National Theatre actors and an invited audience to the Roundhouse Theatre in Camden for the filming of practical workshop sessions, punctuated by open discussion, of six Shakespeare plays. Bogdanov admitted three motives for attempting the experiment: a sense of theoretical isolation; a dissatisfaction with the apparent timelessness of Shakespeare teaching; and an impatience with the BBC's handling of Shakespeare, 'which has done the greatest disservice to Shakespeare in the last twenty-five years'.[30] In the workshops director and actors could be observed constructing sections of a play, experimenting with different possibilities, arguing amongst themselves, involving the live audience. Hand-held cameras shakily recorded the proceedings with odd-angle immediacy and strangeness: other cameras, sound equipment and technicians were visibly present as the practical infrastructure of the dramatic event. The texts are often rigidly interpreted by the director, and sections of the programmes appear to be lectures given by Bogdanov to a passive audience, using the actors as visual aids. And there is no doubt that to some extent the programmes act as mythologising agents: confirming, by an insistence on Shakespeare's *modernity*, the infinite and perpetual universality of his work.[31] Each broadcast begins with the statement: 'Shakespeare is the greatest living playwright'. But the forces of directorial authority and of the universalist ideology itself were inevitably weakened by the open situation: in a context of practical experiment open to question by both actors and audience, the texts became at times musical scores for dramatic improvisation, or battlegrounds for the play of conflicting attitudes, interpretations and ideas.

Agencies of cultural authority in such a context wield far less power than in the achieved finality of a BBC production. Both Jonathan Miller and Michael Bogdanov have very definite views on *The Taming of the Shrew*. Miller sees it as a play advocating marital obedience: 'Shakespeare … underwrote the idea that the state, whether it was the small state of the family or the larger state of the country, required and needed the unquestioned authority of some sort of sovereign'; Bogdanov sees it as a feminist drama, 'showing Petruchio chastened and Kate victorious'.[32] Miller covered the end credits of his production with a Puritan psalm celebrating 'the orderliness and beauty of the family', thus curtailing any potential liberty of the drama to arouse the play of meanings, by imposing the sovereign authority of *scripture*, the written word. Bogdanov's workshop involved a quarrel between Daniel Massey (Petruchio) and Suzanne Bertish (Katherine) disputing whether in the play the man or the woman emerges victorious. Miller, averse to any 'mixing of conventions' in televising theatre, sheared the *Induction* from the play altogether; Bogdanov's workshop (following his production) foregrounded it as a necessary perspective for the play's exploration of sexual politics.[33]

The 'workshop' format can certainly be regarded as an alternative form for the televising of Shakespeare. In place of the monumental stability of a definitive version, the cultural authority of an institutional production, solidly flanked by the apparatus of special occasion, publicity promotion, ancillary introduction, linked publications, we have the provisional, tentative, unfinished debate of the practical rehearsal, and the spectacle of people struggling to make meaning out of Shakespeare. *Shakespeare Lives!*, despite its association with the National Theatre, made no attempt to adapt the constructed television situation to established institutional forms, but rather appropriated Shakespeare into a context familiar enough from other television programmes (such as panel discussions) to give the form a certain accessibility. Where the BBC/Time-Life Series consistently employed the institutional powers of the Corporation to emulate the high culture of a theatrical experience, *Shakespeare Lives!* unashamedly adapted Shakespeare to a specifically televisual form and in doing so, opened up to inspection and debate both the plays and the processes by which meanings are made from them.

It should not be assumed, however, that the televised workshop is an inherently radical site of cultural production. An example of the workshop form institutionalised to the point where any radical energy the medium may possess is dissipated and lost, is the series *Playing Shakespeare*: featuring John Barton, produced by London Weekend Television and broadcast on

Channel Four in 1984. The cultural and ideological provenance of the series is that crucial symbiosis of Cambridge English and Royal Shakespeare defined by Christopher McCullough as 'the Cambridge Connection'.[34] Strictly speaking the sessions filmed and subsequently published in book form were not workshops but discussions between a director and actors. The actors 'read' rather than performed the texts: the context resembling the structured informality of a seminar rather than the active practical experiment of a rehearsal or improvisation. The object of the series, as defined by Trevor Nunn, was the exemplification and illustration of a 'method':

> What the programmes, and now the published texts on the series, reveal, is the method and principle of an approach to acting Shakespeare which has been fundamental to the RSC since it was formed. This approach is not didactic or political or scholastic or literary. It relies a good deal on analysis, but just as much on common sense and pragmatism, and a sense of theatre and character; it attempts to serve the complexities and contradictions of the text, but it is also trying to make the language *work*, and to be alive and exciting in the theatre.[35]

The cultural context invoked here is immediately recognisable: all these principles – the repudiation of ideology, the attempt to combine a 'method' of analysis with a pragmatic 'common sense', the emphasis on a practical methodology for bringing texts to 'living' realisation – can be heard echoing up and down the ideological corridor that leads from Downing College to the banks of the Avon.

John Barton's conception of the series was as a body of 'practical guidance to actors'. The 'practical guidance' offered amounts to a series of 'practical criticism' seminars, in which a motley gallimaufry of selected passages, irresistibly reminiscent of Arnold's 'touchstones', is subjected to detailed verbal and metrical analysis. The texts, or rather the decontextualised gobbets, become concrete embodiments of expressive matter: articulating the character's emotions, the actor's experience, the texture of sensuous reality: '"in sequent toil all forwards do contend": those words capture the swish and chafing of the sea' (Barton, *Playing Shakespeare*, p.108).

Despite the pragmatic common sense approach of this method, its undogmatic, exploratory empiricism, it is carefully directed towards the construction of a myth. The ultimate object of exploration is nothing less than Shakespeare's 'intentions': those elusive properties here conceived not as pearls of high seriousness, but as 'hidden directions', guidance to the actor which 'Shakespeare himself provided'. 'Shakespeare's text is full of hidden hints to the actors. When an actor becomes aware of them he will find that Shakespeare himself starts to direct him.' Barton himself, etched in Trevor Nunn's memory as 'the young man with the Renaissance face' (Nunn, 'Foreword'), is a suitable intermediary for the transmission of these instructions from a dead director. Any actor chilled by the prospect of confrontation with this ghoulish revenant, the director from beyond the grave, can rest assured that nothing harmful or disturbing is likely to be communicated: nothing but reassuring avuncular wisdom and serene humane understanding: 'Shakespeare is timeless in the sense that he anatomises and understands what is in men and women in any age, and what he has to say is always true and real' (Barton, *Playing Shakespeare*, p. 190).

The Shakespeare engendered from this coupling of *Scrutiny* and Stratford is easily recognisable as a manifestation of the Shakespeare myth. It is 'not of an age, but for all time'; its preternatural intelligence and contemplative gaze flicker between the practicalities of production and the immutable truths of human nature, rolling from stage to 'heavens' and back again. John Barton identifies completely with this superhuman monstrosity: Shakespeare, he affirms, did not have a 'political philosophy', only a sense of human nature. Barton, like his fellow director Shakespeare, spurns the quotidian and contemplates the timeless verities of eternal human nature: 'I'm sometimes asked about my own political views. I usually answer that they are Shakespearean ... Shakespeare is neither rightwing nor leftwing in his philosophy and temperament. In political terms he is *wingless*' (Barton, *Playing Shakespeare*, p. 190).

৯

Public controversy about broadcasting has been dominated from the beginning by assumptions about its immense potency as a medium of cultural, social and ultimately political influence and power. The incessant watchfulness of government, Parliament, party politicians and even MI5 over the BBC's appointments and its broadcasts of news and political discussion, a vigilance which has led to acrimonious accusations of political bias, bespeaks a medium of such power that the character of its product, and the mechanisms of its control and accountability are a constant site of ideological struggle and political contestation. Although the Peacock committee[36] disappointed Mrs Thatcher by declining to surrender the BBC immediately to the free play of market forces, its recommendations envisage the ultimate dismantling of the Corporation and the disappearance of the concept of state-financed public service broadcasting. Although the voice of John Reith can still be heard in the land – 'the BBC's problem', affirmed Noel Annan, 'is to re-establish itself as a national Church of culture'[37] – technological developments in television broadcasting, such as cable and satellite, will lead inevitably, as Peacock recognised, to some fundamental revaluation of the BBC. In such a volatile situation we should be clear about our political priorities: should the BBC be defended as a bulwark of liberal-humanist values against the tide of commercialised barbarism? Or is the 'public' the Corporation ultimately 'serves' still that powerful minority extrapolated and extolled by John Reith and by the monarchy as 'the people'?

In 1977 the Annan committee on the future of broadcasting dealt with the right of access to the medium.

There is a right to speak in a free democracy, but it does not follow from this that there is a right to be listened to. I have a right to speak, you have an obligation not to stop me; but you do not have an obligation to listen to me. It does not follow that, because by a flick of the switch you can cut me off and stop listening, that I have a right of access to the medium, since there is a limited amount of time and air space. The claim to speak on it whenever you want is, in effect, a claim to be listened to; and that is an unrealistic demand. (3.14)[38]

The argument is of course Matthew Arnold's: of what value is freedom if the possessor does not know how to use it? As mediated by T.S. Eliot: freedom of speech is futile unless the recipient of that liberty has something of value to say. But who judges such value and such utility? Who decides which utterance is futile and which worthwhile? Socialist politician Tony Benn, in his contribution to the Annan report, drew attention to its articulation of this liberal dilemma: who, by the terms of this common sense view, *does* have the right to have their ideas broadcast? Benn argued that the issue should be shifted, away from a consideration of whether or not programmes were good or serious, balanced or truthful, towards a concern with the medium's ability to allow people to reflect to each other the diversity of their interests and opinions, the nature of their grievances and hopes, the variations and differences between their ideologies. Such a medium, more open to democratic access, would clearly be more effective in expressing and disclosing the contradictions within society, and deeply subversive of the moral certainties that have formed the covert propaganda of the BBC from John Reith to the present day.

Benn's argument is followed in the Annan report by the views of Sir Kenneth Clark, endorsed by the committee (3.16). Clark denies that television debases popular taste: on the contrary it widens people's horizons, 'even whetting their appetites for art and ideas, producing works of dramatic art and familiarising people with great works of literature'. Clark's avuncular liberalism has replaced Reith's moral paternalism but the ideological function of the medium remains curiously unchanged. In a divided society the central institution of communication is controlled by those whose interests lie in reinforcing the concept of a unified commonwealth with a stable and shared system of beliefs and values: the business of broadcasting, says the Annan report, is to produce 'visions of order in a troubled world' (3.2).

I have argued that television production of Shakespeare can disclose radical potentialities only when its forms and methodologies touch those areas of popular participation and democratic access. I have offered the example of the early BBC as a fruitful site of Shakespeare reproduction: although its productions emanated directly from the Reithian policy of 'mixed programming', designed to secure a homogeneous and unified audience, its practice provides a model for the manipulation of Shakespeare into accessible forms relatively free from ideological control. Where television has adapted the Elizabethan drama as in the 1953 *Henry V* or the 1983 first tetralogy by historically based production techniques calculated to deliver those theatrical energies inscribed into the texts by the conditions of their original performance, it has been possible to provoke from them their residual latent content of popular experience. The most productive form yet devised can be represented by *Shakespeare Lives!*, where actual democratic participation (on however limited and selective a basis) becomes a constitutive element of the medium.

Slight as these creative initiatives may appear, they have been rigorously contained: they have developed in the interstices of an agency of cultural production and distribution which invests its power and principal energy in the reproduction of hegemonic cultural discourses. My comparisons between the medium of television and the conventions of the Elizabethan drama should be completed by a comparison of the BBC as an institution with the Renaissance theatre by which Shakespeare's plays were written. A centralised body, close to the heart of political power in the State, financed by a combination of State patronage and a fee-paying clientele, observed by the watchful eye of a government acutely concerned about the politics of its culture, transmits a metropolitan product throughout a supposedly 'united' kingdom. What needs now to be said of the BBC could be applied retrospectively to the institutionalised Elizabethan theatre:

> The key to the BBC lies in its role as the voice or vision of the British nation. As a national institution it institutes an audiovisual impression of national unity wholly at odds with political, historical, economic and social realities. It provides the London government with the possibility of a unified utterance which denies the diffracted constituency of its vast fiefdom ... Linguistic lines of force pulsate outwards from London via education, television, radio and newspapers. While the hegemony of the BBC persists there will be a proper way to speak, a language of transparency and clarity, the voice of pure reason. BBC English is exactly the speech of that vision (Maley, 'Centralisation', p. 36).

Translated into that language, Shakespeare too becomes the voice of that vision. Re-read via the grammar of an alternative, oppositional discourse, Shakespeare can become a strain in the multivocal and pluralistic polyphony of a democratic culture.

CHAPTER TWO

Shakespeare Rescheduled (1998)

(WITH CAROL BANKS)

CADE: But then are we in order when we are
Most out of order.

(*The First Part of the Contention betwixt the two famous
Houses of Yorke and Lancaster,* or *the Second Part of Henry
the Sixth.* 4. 2. 188–9)

SHAKESPEARE'S ENGLISH history plays were originally
composed out of chronological order, *Henry VI Part 2* preceding *Henry VI Part 1,* and all the *Henry VI* plays and *Richard III*
preceding *Richard II,* both *Henry IV* plays and *Henry V.*[1] Hence
the common references to the first and second tetralogies, when
in historical chronology they are the other way around. It seems
highly improbable that in the theatre of their origin the plays
were subsequently staged as 'sequences'; on the contrary, recent
research indicates that each was independently and individually
shaped by contemporary cultural pressures.[2] Certainly in later
theatres they existed in disaggregated form, with plays like
Richard III and *Henry V* used as star-vehicles for the great actor-
managers, whilst the *Henry VI* plays were virtually forgotten.
Nevertheless, the lives and the historical events recalled in these
plays first occurred in chronological sequence, in the seamless
past out of which England's history is written; and, although
cinema continues to produce individual plays in isolation, as

exemplified by film versions of *Richard III* (Olivier, 1955) and *Henry V* (Olivier, 1944 and Branagh, 1992), the historical model of ordering and linking the plays into groups has become the preferred mode of presentation for television productions from *An Age of Kings* (BBC 1960) to *The BBC Television Shakespeare* (BBC/Time-Life 1978-85). The purpose of this essay is to examine the aesthetic and ideological implications of television's rescheduling of individual plays into a grand historical epic or metanarrative.

Television producers are not the first to re-order the plays in historical sequence. When Shakespeare's work was first collected and published in the prestigious 'First Folio' of 1623, the editors of this posthumously printed volume also chose to present the ten plays, catalogued as 'Histories', in their historical order. Here, like the renamed television dramas, *An Age of Kings* (BBC 1960) and *The Wars of the Roses* (BBC 1964), titles of plays which had previously appeared in single quarto format were also altered. For example, the quarto text descriptively entitled: 'The first part of the Contention betwixt the two famous Houses of Yorke and Lancaster, with the death of the good Duke Humphrey: and the banishment and death of the Duke of *Suffolk*, and the Tragicall end of the proud Cardinall of *Winchester*, with the notable Rebellion of *Jake Cade: And the Duke of Yorkes first claime unto the Crowne*', became simply *The Second Part of King Henry the Sixth*. Changing the order of presentation and the titles, immediately creates a new 'literary' position for each play, suggesting not the individuality of specific events, but continuity; an arrangement which also begins to resemble a more 'natural' order, rather than an artificial or aesthetic composition. However, it is important to observe that this orderly grouping of the plays within the 'First Folio', a practice continued in subsequent collected editions,[3] was an editorial, rather than an authorial or theatrical strategy, a change which, first and foremost, satisfied the conditions of printing, particularly of lengthy volumes of collected writing. The Jacobean 'First Folio' came into circulation at a time when printing plays for a reader was a new idea; Elizabethan drama was not a literary genre but still very much an oral/visual art form. Each live performance was, by its very nature, a unique presentation; its form was therefore fluid and unstable, open to free adaptation and interpretation. However, once transformed into the linear printed text, set out on numbered pages in a bound book, that transient art was captured and fixed, permanently pinned down in a form which has more in common with the chronicles of Tudor history than the shared living experience of transitory theatrical performance. Literary editors and critics from Alexander Pope to the present, have examined Shakespeare's plays in terms of the printed text, and earlier this century those history books were brought into closer affiliation with the plays when a group of scholars agreed on a highly influential theory for not only reading the plays in sequence but also interpreting them as a linked series.

During the Second World War E.M.W. Tillyard re-examined those printed play-texts in conjunction with Tudor historiography and came up with a theory based on order, an 'Elizabethan world picture' which he saw reflected in those past works of a bygone, golden age. In *Shakespeare's History Plays*, published in 1944, Tillyard further claimed that 'Shakespeare conceived his second tetralogy as one great unit', and that 'Disregarding the two isolated plays *[King John* and *Henry VIII]*, we can say further that the two tetralogies make a single unit'.[4] This overview won the support of many subsequent scholars,[5] who also examined the texts producing various readings to endorse the notion that the history plays were a linked and integrated series, revealing a broad and complex panorama of national life, unified and balanced into a coherent aesthetic 'order' mirroring the political order of the Elizabethan state. Like the current trend for drama documentaries, the drama, which was created partly from facts, when reassembled to emulate past lives, moved closer to a type of historical 'faction'.

Until the 1950s theatrical performances of the history plays, motivated by the conventions of the 'live' stage (two to three hour individual performances, their success or failure depending on audience response), remained disaggregated; the popularity of individual plays such as *Henry V* and *Richard III* nurtured, in much the same way as their cinematic equivalents, by the opportunity they afforded to star performers to impress the audience with their fine acting abilities. Furthermore, as Richard David has observed, 'The man in the street goes to the theatre for a play, not a political treatise' and he (or she) 'is hardly prepared to stomach a trilogy, much less an "octology"'.[6] But by the mid-century, as lines of communication lengthened and multiplied (railways and radio, telephones, telexes and television), linear sequential interpretations also penetrated performance. In 1951 Anthony Quayle directed the summer season of history plays at Stratford-upon-Avon, setting a precedent for the history 'series' in performance with the *Richard II* to *Henry V* 'tetralogy' performed from March to July in historical sequence, the programme for *Richard II* boldly consolidating contemporary literary theory, claiming that 'It is generally agreed that the four plays of this season's historical cycle form a tetralogy and were planned by Shakespeare as one great play'. Added to this, Quayle's own remarks concerning the 'ignorance' he associates with the previous theatrical mode of presenting the plays in isolation, suggest that the sequential interpretation, developed in the loftier heights of academia, is somehow enlightening:

> ... it seemed to us that the great epic theme of the Histories had become obscured through years of presenting the plays singly.
> ... Successful theatrical practice over a great number of years had stealthily built a mountain of misrepresentation and surrounded it with a fog of ignorance.[7]

Not surprisingly, Richard David, reviewing the plays, commented that 'Everything in Anthony Quayle's production was focused on continuity, on the connexions and the likenesses between the plays, and their differences were studiously toned down'.[8] But whereas theatre relied on a minority of extremely dedicated

spectators to purchase all four tickets across the season, television
had a ready-made audience and established success with both
'serials' and 'series', so the next step was easily made from theatrical tetralogy to television's first epic octology *An Age of Kings*
(BBC 1960), produced by Peter Dews and directed by Michael
Hays. The eight discrete plays, reassembled into fifteen 60–90
minute, weekly instalments, were now transformed into a continuous, all embracing metanarrative of English medieval history,
and brought within the reach of a large percentage of the population via the television screen. Once the sequential formula was
established, future televised performances followed suit. In 1964
the BBC's Michael Barry enlisted Royal Shakespeare Company
directors Peter Hall and John Barton, to produce a three part
series of the first tetralogy (an adaption of the RSC's *Henry VI,
Edward IV* and *Richard III*), in which Shakespeare's three *Henry
VI* plays and *Richard III*, were, like the Dews/Hays production,
chronologically reordered, suitably cut, modified and renamed
The Wars of the Roses (BBC 1964).

   This infiltration of historical and printed modes into the
drama was taken a stage further when video recordings added
permanence and repeatability to television productions. When
the BBC/Time-Life Shakespeare (1978–85) was in the making,
these considerations were of particular significance. The original
producer, Cedric Messina, explained that: 'The guiding principle
… is to make the plays, in permanent form, accessible to audiences throughout the world'[9] so that the spectator 'can go to the
screen and see the whole panorama of the historical plays, leading
one into another'.[10] To tighten those sequential links between one
production (or video recording) and the next, flashbacks to the
previous 'episodes' silently open each play, e.g. *Henry IV Part
Two* beginning with two clips from *Richard II* – Richard handing
the crown to Bolingbroke and Richard's murder, followed by
two clips from *Henry IV Part One* – Henry IV at prayer and the
mortal combat between Prince Hal and Hotspur. Returning the
plays to the popular oral/visual medium of film provides an

opportunity for liberation from the fixity of the printed text, a move successfully achieved in certain cinematic versions of Shakespeare's plays, such as Akira Kurosawa's *Throne of Blood* (1957), and Peter Hall's *A Midsummer Night's Dream* (1968).[11] But the enchaining metanarrative structure imposed by television on the history plays succeeds rather in closing off possibilities for radical interpretation. Furthermore, as Messina rightly observed, video recordings are, like printing, a 'permanent form', and permanence lends authority to that enchaining metanarrative, authority which is easily confused with definitive 'truth' and further closure. To appreciate the way that subtle re-ordering so effectively denies alternative interpretations, we need to examine the narrative structure itself.

The components of any narrative may be divided into 'story' and 'discourse'. 'Story' covers *what* is depicted (characters, settings, happenings, etc.) and the 'discourse' is *how* those components are presented, the means by which the story is communicated to the reader/spectator.[12] The selection and ordering of events within the narrative (the plotting) is part of the discourse, being the means by which the reader/spectator is made aware of what happens. The plot may follow a resolved, causal pattern – one event leading to the next – or it may be one of revelation, in which the function of the discourse is not to supply answers/resolutions, but merely to reveal a particular state of affairs. When the history plays are interpreted collectively, each play becomes a 'story' component (a group of characters and events) in a wider narrative. If these are then arranged chronologically, the temporal linking produces a strong sense of unravelling in terms of cause and effect, in other words a resolved plot; whereas if they are randomly arranged, the causal element diminishes and connections appear in other ways. Resolved plots follow a linear structure, being predominantly a chain of events; revealed plots, a characteristic of much 'modernist' fiction, are more amorphous and do not propel the reader/spectator forward towards a final closure but invite his/her participation in the

work. The editors and directors who rearrange the plays in linear
chronology are therefore manipulating a resolved meaning by the
very structure they impose upon the diverse components, a structure which denies the comparative freedom of a revealed plot and
with it the possibility of radical interpretation. Alan Sinfield
points out how a belief in 'order' can even unite quite different
interpretations, as was the case with the Barton/Hall production
The Wars of the Roses, in which the apparently opposing views of
Tillyard and Jan Kott [13] become 'two sides of the same conservative coin'.[14] Hall said that his direction was guided by a belief in
Tillyard's 'Elizabethan World Picture': 'All Shakespeare's thinking,
whether religious, political or moral, is based on complete acceptance of this concept of order'; yet his equal conviction that
'Shakespeare always knew that man in action is basically an animal'[15] supports Kott's view of 'a cruel social order in which the
vassals and superiors are in conflict with each other, the kingdom
is ruled like a farm, and falls prey to the strongest'.[16] As Sinfield
observes, the combination of these views is 'powerfully conservative' in so far as it 'offers no hope for humanity and no analysis of
the sources and structures of injustice'.[17] In spite of Kott's repudiation of Tillyard's view, his image of history as the 'implacable
roller' which 'crushes everybody and everything'[18] leaves no hope
for escape from the causal chain.

The structural linearity imposed by editors and producers in
support of their political/ideological convictions, is certainly
compatible with the plays in printed format but it is far less significant in oral/visual art forms. Traditional oral narratives (still
evident in ballads, fairy tales, nursery rhymes, myths and legends)
depend on human memory for retention and are therefore structured, like poetry, around balanced patterns, repetitions, antithesis, and thematic links.[19] These connections do not merely move
along a horizontal line of causal enchainment; there are vertical
links, reversals and circular rotations. It is worth noting here that
certain play titles: *The Life and Death of King John* and *The Life of
Henry the Fifth*, suggest that 'life' itself is the guiding principle

here and within the plays 'life' is repeatedly described in circular patterns: ' ... life did ride upon a dial's point,/Still ending at the arrival of an hour' (*Henry IV Part One* 5. 2. 83–4). Considering the history plays collectively within an oral network, vertical parallels may certainly be drawn between kings of the same name, such as Richard III and Richard II, and perhaps it is more than a coincidence that the plays *Richard III* and *Richard II* were both printed in quarto in the same year – 1597. These kings then invite comparison, the sinful Richard III, a debased, but skilful schemer, offsetting the weak, yet saintly Richard II, as regal as pride and piety permits, each thus achieving definition by contrast with the other. Similarly, and more overtly, the rebel Jack Cade in *The First part of the Contention*, is actually compared, within the play, to the hero king Henry V:

> Is Cade the son of Henry the Fifth
> That thus you do exclaim you'll go with him?
> Will he conduct you through the heart of France
> And make the meanest of you earls and dukes? (4. 8. 189–192)

Once identified on a parallel scale, further equations begin to emerge. For example, Jack Cade denounces literacy in favour of orality:

> Away! Burn all the records of the realm. My mouth shall be the
> Parliament of England.   (4.7. 12–14)

Although Henry V is far from illiterate, he not only admits his inadequacy when it comes to rhetoric but forcefully justifies his own plain speech:

> I am glad thou canst speak no better English, for if thou couldst,
> thou wouldst find me such a plain king that thou wouldst think I
> had sold my farm to buy my crown ...
> ... before God, Kate, I cannot ... gasp out my eloquence ...
> I speak to thee plain soldier ... take a fellow of plain and
> uncoined constancy, for he perforce must do thee right, because
> he hath not the gift to woo in other places ...
>
> (*Henry V*, 5.2. 122–156)

In this speech alone the linking of 'king', 'soldier' and 'fellow' are made by repetition of the epithet 'plain'. The parallels drawn between the rebel Cade and Henry V seriously question the theory that, to the Elizabethans, Henry Monmouth was 'the ideal representative of order and security'.[20] Instead, the effect is one of levelling, a view more obviously conveyed in the quarto play of *Henry V* (*The Chronicle History of Henry the fift, With his battell fought at Agin Court in France.* Together with *Auntient Pistoll* [1600]), where Henry is less of a hero in the epic and historicist mode, more of a gentle gamester:

> For when cruelty and lenitie play for a Kingdome,
> The gentlest gamester is the sooner winner.[21]

In this play the distinct plebianising and carnivalisation of the monarch effectively sets monarch and man face to face in a ritual enactment of that myth of equality which underlies the comic romance motif of 'the king disguised';[22] and here the orgiastic festival of violence, celebrated on the field of Agincourt, aligns Henry very closely with the man from Eastcheap – Pistoll:

> *Kin* … What new alarum is this?
> Bid every soldier kill his prisoner.
> *Pist.* Couple gorge.[23]

Notably, Pistoll's name, like that of Jack Cade, is also given a place of prominence in the play's title.

Of course, a strong case for interpreting the histories as linked sequences is the presence of the word 'part' in certain original titles, but even here the various parts do not necessarily follow in temporal sequence. The first *Henry IV* play, originally entitled *The History of Henry the Fourth* (Stationer's Register 1598), includes various episodes depicting Henry IV's son, Prince Hal: his involvement in wayward dalliances at Eastcheap and Gad's Hill; the battle of Shrewsbury in which he replaces Hotspur as the chivalric hero; and finally his reformation as, in the closing scenes, he takes up his regal position to climb with his brother 'to the highest of the field' (5.4. 159), before being united with his father 'To fight with Glendower and the Earl of March' (5.5.40). On the Elizabethan stage, this clearly proved a popular play, not least due to the creation of the fictitious character Falstaff, who brings a riot of carnival colour to the events depicted, so much so that, as legend has it, the queen herself requested to see another play showing Falstaff in love.[24] After Falstaff's second appearance in the non-historical play *The Merry Wives of Windsor* (where the women are allowed to get the better of him), he was again returned to the stage for a second involvement with the prince. However, *The Second Part of Henry Fourth* does not pick up from where the earlier play left off. Instead it returns to the battle of Shrewsbury via the allegorical figure 'Rumour', who reminds the audience, in a fine piece of double talk, not to believe what they may have heard: 'From Rumour's tongues / They bring smooth comforts false, worse than true wrongs' (Induction, 39–40). The audience soon learns that Hal is not, as the first play had led us to believe, reformed, but is still cavorting around with his low-life comrades. The play goes on to repeat a similar pattern of events to those previously enacted – Hal up to no good in the tavern; Hal proving his royal worth; and finally Hal once more taking up his regal position, this final point of departure having indeed moved on a year or so to effect the death of Henry IV so that Hal may be crowned and this time make a more positive rejection of his unruly friend Falstaff. The second part considered in this way does not roll on from the first, but doubles back, attempting to repeat that earlier successful performance.

This repetitive technique is successfully employed in numerous television 'series' where a main character, or group of characters repeat similar 'adventures' in each successive programme. But the pattern was certainly used in oral myths and legends, such as the adventures of Robin Hood and the tales of King Arthur. Non-sequential structuring still shaped manuscript or early printed collections of stories and Murray Roston cites the widely read *Legenda Aurea* by Jacabus de Voraigne (c.1297) as an example of a collection of saints stories which 'lack any co-ordinating thread or rational order other than their shared didactic purpose'.[25] Alternatively, a collection of stories, such as Chaucer's *The Canterbury Tales* (c.1387), could use a particular scene/setting – the road to Canterbury – as an organising framework. This contextual structuring was similarly used in the visual arts of the early Renaissance. The sculptor Ghiberti united his 'continuous narration' (episodes of a story that are disparate in time and place shown as though occurring simultaneously) of Jacob and Esau (*Gates of Paradise* 1452, Florence) by means of an architectural perspective – an arched loggia.[26] In terms of two or three part narratives, such as the Henry plays, it is illuminating to compare them with other grouped visual representations such as diptych or triptych paintings.[27] The *Wilton Diptych* (c.1400), previously at Wilton House, home of the Earl of Pembroke to whom the 'First Folio' was dedicated, comprises two separate images: an earthly grouping of the monarch (Richard II) and saints (St John, St Edward the Confessor and St Edmund) and a spiritual revelation of the Virgin, Christ child and a host of angels. The frames are not chronologically linked, this is not a case of Richard's arrival in heaven; they share neither the same scale nor the same space/setting but are brought into conjunction thematically as a celebration of Richard's piety. In another more complex example of pictorial narrative, Piero della Francesca's *Legend of the True Cross* (1452–66, S. Francesco chapel, Arezzo), it has been suggested that the Renaissance fascination with mathematics[28] could supply the linking formula for the random composition of the ten scenes which make up this fresco narrative; a cycle which 'abounds with such echoes and reflections – thematic, liturgical, and formal – in a dense network that crosses horizontally, vertically and diagonally' so that 'the chronological thread of the story, its succession in history, becomes lost in this web'. This apparently mysterious arrangement is unlocked by applying a formula based on a Pythagorean number theory.[29] As these examples demonstrate, the co-ordinating links which can serve to unite components in a narrative are far more diverse than the historicist obsession with temporal causality, an ordering which clings to a sense of 'natural' clock time as opposed to more psychological, thematic, theological or scientific linkings.

The effortless acceptances of apparent 'naturalism' in historical ordering is itself enhanced by television, accustomed as we are to the 'natural' presentation of current news programmes (tomorrow's history), documentaries, chat shows, etc. Jonathan Miller, who succeeded Cedric Messina as producer of *The BBC Television Shakespeare* plays, accepted this as the basis for his 'naturalistic' approach, maintaining that 'as soon as you put Shakespeare on that box where ... people are accustomed to seeing naturalistic events presented, you are more or less obliged to present the thing as naturally as you can'.[30] Naturalistic settings, 'authentic' medieval costumes and a moving camera which roams in and out of the scenes, are amongst the devices employed to create the illusion of reality. Perhaps the most powerful convention of all for encouraging the sense of naturalness in terms of temporal continuity, and one adopted by all producers of the combined performances of the plays on television, is the use of the same actors for characters who appear in different plays, 'ageing' them in accordance with the imaginary passage of time. Reviewing *An Age of Kings*, Milton Crane noted how 'Robert Hardy's Prince Hal, grew visibly through *Henry IV* toward the magnificence of *Henry V*.[31] A notable exception within these overall naturalistic productions has been considered in Chapter One, Jane Howell's treatment of the first tetralogy. Aware of the multiplicity of potential meanings, Howell refused to accept Miller's insistence on naturalism. Using a bare stage with minimal, emblematic props and scenery, a group of actors operating as an *ensemble*, doubling parts to prevent the illusionary identification of actor with character, Howell managed to highlight the 'artificiality' of her productions. However, even when the viewer is made patently aware that this is 'but a play', these attempts at a radical interpretation are still held within the restricting chain of temporal causality, conveying that orthodox 'providential' view which begins with a crime against God's judgement – the deposition of a rightful king (Richard II), followed by a series of bloody battles until the Tudor king (Henry VII) is lawfully restored. What these epic productions are doing, under cover of an apparently 'natural' ordering of time, is channelling the viewer to accept implicitly a deliberate construct designed to convey a particular interpretation, an interpretation which, far from being the definitive course of history, is no more than a singular point of view from a specific ideological standpoint. The singularity of that interpretation is evident in the very fact that events are seen in succession, one at a time; whereas interpretations from multiple viewpoints overlap, occur simultaneously or conflict. The ideologies informing that singular view are traditionalist/politically conservative, hence that unbroken chain of historical causation which denies radical change, digression or individual initiative. In establishing authority for that view television offers more than the opportunity for a naturalistic presentation.

Television, specifically the BBC, developed from radio, sound preceding pictures; whereas cinema's roots are in photography which became 'moving pictures' before sound was finally incorporated. Pictures may 'move the soul of the beholder',[32] but language is the means by which knowledge is transmitted. Where cinema continues to function, like theatre, primarily as a source of entertainment, television (together with radio) fulfils a wider role in society, as a major means of communication and is arguably the most important medium for disseminating information about the outside world, bringing news and information directly into the home. The annual television licence fee is in part justified by this 'public service'. Regulations governing both the BBC and the IBA reveal their pursuit of 'public service broadcasting': 'to provide radio and television services for the dissemination of information, education and entertainment' and to ensure and maintain programme quality and standards.[33] Unfortunately, members of 'the public' are not all satisfied by the same values, and since broadcasting is a heavily selected interpretation of art and events, the question is whose interests are actually being served by the system? This was a point specifically raised during the Falklands War when television reports, attempting to remain impartial, were criticised by Margaret Thatcher for that very impartiality:

> Many people are very concerned indeed that the case for our British forces is not being put over fully and effectively. I understand that there are times when it seems that we and the Argentines are being treated almost as equals ... [34]

The 'epic' interpretation of Shakespeare's history plays satisfies the interests of the culturally and politically conservative. Backed by traditional academia, it supports the mythical ideal of Shakespeare as the most celebrated of English authors – poet and dramatist, capable of conceiving and creating a national epic as did the great writers of ancient Greece and Rome, Homer and Virgil. Furthermore, it suggests that Shakespeare endorsed the ideologies of the Elizabethan ruling élite, or at the very least saw no alternatives, and subsequently denies the opportunity to peel back that glossy Elizabethan film, and to hear the voices of discontent that were already being raised, and which culminated in civil war only twenty six years after Shakespeare's death. The basis for this argument, the 'providential theory', is of course retrospective in outlook, looking back to an older social order, justifying hereditary privilege and opposing change. Jonathan Miller, discussing BBC/Time-Life series, makes exactly this point when he maintains that Shakespeare was 'looking backwards over the chaos of the previous century during the Wars of the Roses ... And he comes down on the side of an orderly society ruled by an efficient sovereign'.[35] The political outcome of these interpretations is to gild the pillars of state power with cultural authority. But seen in this context it becomes clear that, where television may lend authority to the metanarrative structure, the medium itself does not dictate this view of Shakespeare's history plays, but rather the ideologies of those responsible for their production. As this sense of continuous transmission is recognised instinctively when we talk about 'watching television' rather than watching a particular unit within that 'flow'. When plays are slotted into what Raymond Williams defined as the 'sequence' or 'flow' of broadcasting,[36] this continuum, rhythm and duration take on new significance. Hence the de-composition of the meta-narrative into convenient parts, most notably the fifteen parts of *An Age of Kings*, and the compression created by cutting, in order to fit the events into hourly, ninety-minute or two-hourslots. Peter Saccio points out how in the BBC/Time-Life productions, the rhythm is altered, stretching out time by splitting scenes – for example in *Richard II* when the colloquy of Northumberland, Willoughby and Ross is depicted in a different location from the death of Gaunt (Act 2, scene 1), and condensing the passage of time via camera dissolves – occurring five times during Richard's prison soliloquy. These compressions and decompressions of narrative time, made possible by filming techniques, create, in these productions, more space for history 'to peep through the interstices'.[37] In this instance the nature of the medium has been used to satisfy the historicist interpretation, but it could equally be utilised to very different ends. The television viewer is, for example, perfectly adapted to receiving a stream of fragmented, totally unrelated, presentations within the flow of transmission. A typical evening's viewing (without changing channels) moves from news to a satire on the day's news, to a documentary about Ireland, to a sitcom, then a 'behind the scenes' view of news-making, followed by one of a detective series, then a psychological thriller film (Monday 20 March 1995, 7.00 pm – 12.35 am, Channel 4); all this further fragmented by the intervention of grouped, disaggregated commercials. To avoid the commercials, viewers can, and do, switch over and pick up a fragment from a programme on one of the other channels. As a collection of disparate units the combination of these programmes resembles a 'revealed' rather than a 'resolved' mode of plotting.

When Shakespeare's plays were first transposed onto silent film they too were short 'extracts' – Beerbohm Tree's *tableaux vivants* from *King John* (1899) and the shipwreck scene from *The Tempest* (Tree/Urban 1903). These experimental films were predominantly 'visualisations' from Shakespeare and were therefore much closer to pictorial art. In terms of historical drama, Tree's pioneering work continues to reverberate in the disaggregated approach and strong visual emphasis on cinematic productions of Shakespeare's histories, but it is a far cry from television's mode of presentation. Television, backed by video, now impregnates the oral/visual mode with both the authority and the permanence of print, whilst the 'factual' element within the plays encourages an easy acceptance of naturalistic and chronologically ordered presentations. From a post-modern perspective, in which art is recognised as artifice, it is important to see the picture within the frame. When Shakespeare's history plays are arranged to resemble 'real life', the danger is that the framing hand, manipulating those events towards their resolution, seems to be, as Stephen Dedalus explained, 'like the god of creation, ... invisible, refined out of existence',[38] an idea far removed from the overt artificiality of the Elizabethan theatre. Television drama is as much a contrived construct as live theatre, and in a society which is increasingly returning to visual/oral modes of communication, television does offer an opportunity to represent pre-print art forms in a way which could open up interpretative possibilities. Instead of channelling the viewer blindly down a particular ideological alley, television could reveal further potential in Shakespeare's plays via their original order, which was 'Most out of order'.

PART TWO

Film

CHAPTER THREE

Shakespeare and Cinema (1985, 1991)

ॐ

W HEREAS THE BBC TV Shakespeare series could be regarded as a characteristic expression of the cultural policies of the producing corporation, cinematic reproduction of Shakespeare constitutes at best a marginal dimension of film history. The relation between 'Shakespeare' and 'film' consists in an exchange of cultural authority between institutions in a reciprocal process. The repute of cinema art and of the film industry can be enhanced by their capacity to incorporate Shakespeare; the institution of Shakespeare itself benefits from that transaction by a confirmation of its persistent universality. Shakespeare films exist on that important but peripheral fringe of cinematic production, where the values of high art can be held to justify or compensate for any lack of commercial success, and they can scarcely be regarded as central to the mainstream practice and development of the cinema.

This essay has no space to attempt a general survey of Shakespeare films;[1] but will instead confine itself to two basic problems: the position of Shakespeare films within what has been defined as the ideological function of the cinema in society and the existing status and potential value of films within the dominant practices of literary education.

Writing from within the embattled domain of 'Literature' teaching and criticism, we are likely to assume that any translation of a Shakespeare text into a 'live' dramatic form – theatrical performance, film adaptation, television production – will automatically constitute a progressive act. Such translation seems inevitably to entail a liberation of the *play*, a text for reproduction or recreation in performance, from the fetished commodity of the *text*; and any move to challenge the hegemony of that dominant form of ideological oppression must, surely, be welcomed.

Theatrical, film and television productions have always been accorded a place and a potential value within the broad conspectus of a literary education: the question is what place, and what value? Are such things ancillary to the essential critical labour, marginal divisions to the study of texts? Traditional literary studies must keep them peripheral, since when they become a central focus they tend to displace the text from its central role in constituting the nature of the subject; tend to render the discipline itself unstable, open to question, vulnerable to change. Useful evidence of the tension created when film is introduced into the institution of Literature can be found in GCE 'O' level examiners' reports (I offer a few instances from many examples):

> Imaginative interpretations of texts can be misleading. The visual impact of films and productions of plays was often stronger than the impact of Shakespeare's or Hardy's words.[2]
> Films and stage-productions are not always entirely helpful. Lady Macduff bathing her son, Macbeth's soldiers attacking her maids, Lady Macbeth leaping from the battlements, Macbeth's mutilated body scattered across the stage, were so commonplace that it seemed fortunate that productions of *The Crucible* were less easily available. (1973, p. 9)
> … most candidates appeared to know *Macbeth* well. Some, however, were handicapped by having seen a film version … candidates should remember that it is Shakespeare's text which is being examined. (1977, p. 9)

'Literature' here encounters 'Film' as a subversive influence to be resisted, marginalised or suppressed. Is the adoption of

Shakespeare by the cinematic medium in educational practice, if not in the commercial cinema, inherently radical?

Catherine Belsey, in a very interesting article,[3] proposes exactly the opposite: in her argument, both the literary text and a theatrical production under Elizabethan stage conditions are potentially productive of plurality of meaning, whereas films operate to close the plural work into a single dimension of significance:

> In the Elizabethan theatre there is no proscenium arch, no painted back-drop defining a setting in perspective, but a stage projected outwards into the auditorium, with the audience placed on at least three sides of it and possibly four. There is no single place to which the action is addressed and from which it is intelligible. The introduction after 1660 of the proscenium theatre with prospective backdrops radically changed the relationship between the audience and the stage ...
> ... Film is the final realisation of the project of prospective staging. The framed rectangle contains a world which is set out as the single object of the spectator's gaze, displayed in order to be known from a single point of view ... Through the intervention of the camera, which monitors what we see and therefore what we know, the film collects up meanings which may be lying around in the text, and streamlines them into one single, coherent interpretation which it fixes as inescapable. It arrests the play of possible meanings and presents its brilliant rectangle full of significance to and from a specific place, a single and at the same time inevitable point of view.

This passage represents a body of opinion which forms, to my original thesis, the antithesis: that film is an inherently *conservative* medium, which inevitably exercises a despotic ideological control over the spectator's responses, closing off the work's potentiality for multiplicity of significance, depriving the audience of an opportunity to participate in a collaborative construction of meaning. 'Film', in the words of another writer, 'overwhelms the mind with a relentless progression of visual and auditory impulses ... all other arts liberate the imagination, film entraps it.'[4] In terms of this latter view, the medium of film itself can only be an invisible, apparently innocent communicator of ideology. Like the naturalist stage, it purports to provide the spectator with a transparent window on to experience: isolated in the darkness of an auditorium she or he is overwhelmed with an enormous concentration of visual imagery insistently signifying its irreducible reality. Belsey offers as illustrations two films, both of which are said to offer ideology a free, unhampered passage: Joseph L. Mankiewicz's *Julius Caesar* (1953) transmits the liberal dilemma of a bourgeois democratic society; while the *King Lear* (1970) of Peter Brook communicates a 'theoretical nihilism': '... like *Julius Caesar*, this film also makes a political statement: that the struggle for change, however heroic, is doomed in a world where all law, morality and justice are finally illusory'.[5] Mankiewicz's film is of course a piece of thoroughgoing film naturalism, alternating close-ups of the main characters with long-shots of crowd scenes, all played against a 'realistic' Roman background. Belsey acknowledges, in an enthusiastic critique, that the cinematic techniques of *King Lear* are stylistically very different: she lists the grainy black-and-white photography, stylised acting, direct addresses to camera, lightning changes of focus, rapid superimpositions, violations of screen direction. She could have added the Brechtian titles, the absence of music, the distorted images, zoom-fades, blurred visions, surreal apparitions, elliptic camera-work and disjointed editing – all devices which estrange the film's techniques from naturalism and from familiar screen conventions. Can a film constructed from such alienating, deconstructive devices really be a vehicle for the smooth and uninterrupted passage of ideology? Can such discordant techniques really operate to naturalise ideology, obediently miming its chosen language?

Consider Brook's handling of a particularly complex dramatic moment, Gloucester's attempted suicide. Grigori Kozintsev in his film of the play felt that this scene was essentially a theatrical gesture, and avoided it by cutting. Brook with Beckett and Jan Kott in the background, embraced the moment as a central thematic and dramatic focus of the work.

> The director duplicates in cinematic terms Shakespeare's blend of blatant stage artifice and imaginative reality … a long shot shows Edgar and Gloucester struggling along a flat plain. But then, in a series of tight, low-angle close-ups, Edgar and Gloucester seem to climb. The sound of the waves in the distance accords with Edgar's description, and following film convention it makes us imagine an off-screen reality. Set on 'the extremest verge', Gloucester bids farewell to poor Tom, and his final speech of despair is filmed in low-angle close-up … as he falls forward, however, Brook jolts us with an illusion-shattering cut to an extreme overhead long-shot. From this godlike perspective, we watch a tiny old man take a silent pratfall on a barren stretch of sand. (Jorgens, *Shakespeare on Film*, p.240)

The complex effects of this filmic montage cannot adequately be summarised either in terms of Belsey's 'political statement', or of Jorgen's 'absurdist pantomime'. The director has certainly composed and edited his shots to expose the distinction between Gloucester's physical tumble and his psychological fall down mountains of the mind; and the final perspective is that of a god dispassionately watching a wanton boy kill flies. But the effect of, for example, the low-angle close-up of Gloucester's face (described by Jorgens as 'one of the most savagely beautiful shots of a human face ever put on film'), a frame from which the character towers over the spectator in the tragic dignity of suffering, is *complicated* but not *negated* by the jump-cut to an overhead long-shot of his pathetic fall. Moreover, the fracturing of naturalist conventions increases the spectator's awareness of the camera as a constructive device, not a window opening on reality, but a mobile and changing point-of-view which can choose to record in a spirit of empathy or of alienation. The primary function of alienating devices, in this film or any other, is to intensify the viewer's awareness of the mechanisms by which this simulated reality is being produced; to impede the free transmission of ideology by discouraging unconscious, empathetic involvement and encouraging a vigilant and self-conscious curiosity. Belsey's identification of film with naturalist staging, though suggestive, is potentially misleading. Though the proscenium-arch perspective stage is very obviously a *selector* of reality, it can only *appear* to be an innocent *constitutor* of the reality: the spectator's point of vision is fixed, the access to the stage's simulated reality circumscribed, the window on to experience absolutely static. The film camera, by contrast, can do either: it can, like the proscenium arch, efface itself in a privileging of its object, constituting reality as objective in the illusionistic manner of naturalism; or it can, by violating those naturalist conventions, by emphasising and exploiting its mobility, call the spectator's attention to the mechanisms of its own perception. Without employing alienation devices, the naturalist stage can *only* offer itself as the *premise* of a simulated reality; the film can be seen to operate as a moving *commentary* on its object, releasing the viewer from the tyranny of empathetic illusion to a freer consideration of reality and of the artifice which produces it.

Considering Shakespeare films in the light of this most fundamental distinction in the whole of film theory – between naturalistic, illusionist cinema and its opposite – we can conclude that certain filmed adaptations of the plays operate simply as vehicles for the transmissions of ideology. Other films block, deflect or otherwise 'work on' ideology in order partially to disclose its mechanisms. The same method of evaluation will reveal which films are potentially more valuable for mobilisation in the educational context; and which can only work to reinforce and familiarise conventional attitudes to Shakespeare. The object of this essay is not to attempt such evaluation across a wide range of films but rather to suggest, with the help of particular illustrations, methods of procedure and analysis appropriate to such investigation.

In addition to describing the formal characteristics of the medium, some account must be taken, in however abstract a fashion, of the audience itself: which is not, after all, entirely created by the particular work of art it happens to be witnessing. A film of Shakespeare is never experienced in a total vacuum because of the ubiquity, the universality of Shakespeare as a cultural phenomenon. A film's 'arrested play of meanings' will enter into conflictual or co-operative relationship with certain ideological premises, certain cultural assumptions, certain definite levels of knowledge. The school students rebuked by the JMB examiners were witnessing a film *in the light of* some knowledge of the play as literary text. The film may be experienced in a context of other encounters with the play – a TV or theatrical production perhaps, or another film (most of the 'great' Shakespeare plays have been filmed several times). Or the film may simply reinforce or subvert an inherited cultural concept of 'Shakespeare' – the familiar associations of costume drama, perspective staging, unintelligible plots, projected delivery. It is this body of assumptions that an effective film transliteration is likely to subvert: clashing with the spectator's preconceptions to produce a liberating dialectic, to foster that very 'play of meanings' which art can press ideology to deliver.

✍

I have chosen to concentrate my analysis on two examples of ideology-resistant Shakespeare film treatment: Akira Kurosawa's *Throne of Blood* (1957) and Peter Hall's 1969 production of *A Midsummer Night's Dream*. In relation to the latter, a useful comparison is provided by an earlier film version of *A Midsummer Night's Dream*, directed by Max Reinhardt and William Dieterle, made in Hollywood and released in 1935. The lavish, opulent and operatic productions of Max Reinhardt dominated the German theatre in the 1920s, before the radical and innovative productions of the young Marxist writers and directors, such as Brecht and Piscator, began to alter the shape of theatrical culture in the

Weimar Republic. Reinhardt was opposed to what he thought of as *literary* forms of drama, particularly naturalism, which in some ways resembled the novel in its realistic characterisation and narrative. He thought the production of a play should be a theatre event, a visual, aural and technical action which the audience would experience directly through the senses. Reinhardt also thought that theatre should be 'a meeting ground for all the arts', a combination of space, light, music, design, acting, mime, dance and the spoken word. In some ways Reinhardt's theatrical conceptions were akin to the 'pure art' of the Aesthetic movement; in other ways they were parallel with Modernism. Unlike the bohemian artists of the 1890s and the great pioneers of Modernism, Reinhardt was a popular artist; his productions, elaborate and expensive commercial enterprises, toured around the world as packaged samples of the best in German theatrical culture.

Reinhardt's forté was the extravagant, elaborate spectacle, composed by the director acting as a kind of theatrical magician. His stage production of *A Midsummer Night's Dream* was choreographed to Mendelssohn's music, played and danced within elaborate sets. The 'dream' element of the play was conceived and realised as a species of escapist fantasy:

> In Shakespeare's lovely fantasy, I have always seen, above all, a cheering, hopeful reminder that since Life itself is a dream, we can escape it through our dreams within a dream. When stark reality weighs too heavily upon us, an all-wise Providence provides deliverance. Every one has a secret corner into which he can retire and find refuge in Fancy. "A Midsummer Night's Dream" is an invitation to escape reality, a plea for the glorious release to be found in sheer fantasy.[6]

Here the problematical relationship between 'stark reality' and 'dream' is mediated by the intervention of a god-like director, who in the guise of an 'all-wise providence' smooths the reality-burdened spectator into the glorious release of fantasy.

Reinhardt's film version of *A Midsummer Night's Dream* bears many resemblances to the Warner Brothers musicals of the 1930s, and shares with them a common ideology. The specific historical conditions in which both film and spectator were produced (the German Weimar Republic or the America of the Depression) are projected as an inescapable condition of 'stark reality' that can be transcended or evaded in the pursuit of a self-evidently superior fantasy-world of beauty, pleasure and delight. That complex Renaissance sense of the shifting and ambivalent relations between 'reason' and 'fantasy', articulated in Theseus's famous speech –

> THESEUS
> I never may believe
> These antique fables, nor these fairy toys.
> Lovers and madmen have such seething brains,
> Such shaping fantasies, that apprehend
> More than cool reason ever comprehends.
> The lunatic, the lover, and the poet
> Are of imagination all compact.
> One sees more devils than vast hell can hold.
> That is the madman. The lover, all as frantic,
> Sees Helen's beauty in a brow of Egypt.
> The poet's eye, in a fine frenzy rolling,
> Doth glance from heaven to earth, from earth to heaven.
> And, as imagination bodies forth
> The forms of things unknown, the poet's pen
> Turns them to shapes, and gives to airy nothing
> A local habitation and a name.   (V.1.2–17)

– is here reductively confined to the simplicity of a post-Romantic retreat into the cultivated illusion of 'Fancy'.

Taking Theseus's meditation on imagination as a starting point, A Midsummer Night's Dream would appear to be an ideal subject for film adaptation, using exploratory techniques of film narrative and representation to throw the relations between art and artifice, reality and illusion, into a vigorous and liberating visual play. But in Reinhardt's film, Athens is no less of a fantasy than the forest. The civilisation of the city is presented in elaborate visual spectacle as a fantasy landscape, in which minor domestic misunderstandings occur in an atmosphere of romantic comedy:

> The notes of disharmony sounded pose no real threat in the overall atmosphere of triumph and celebration (Jorgens, *Shakespeare on Film*, p.40)

Jorgen's musical metaphor ('notes of disharmony') calls attention to the operatic quality of this film, its dramatic incident and visual narrative choreographed to a musical score. Jorgens goes further, proposing that the film can be regarded as a kind of 'tone-poem' which has actually shaped its visual representations in musical terms:

> The total graphic feeling is like a flow of bright palace crescendos, dusky forest cadenzas, pizzicato glimpses of glistening dewdrops, and large passages of mysterious and lovely moonlit creatures – the whole thoroughly and ornamentally orchestrated for the eye. (Jorgens, *Shakespeare on Film*, p.40)

Here the film is being interpreted as a kind of Wagnerian music-drama; and it is true that Reinhardt's stage practice often seemed to aspire to the totally integrated aesthetic completeness of a perfect work of art. Jorgens on the other hand argues that the film is more complex than Reinhardt's own description of it as a playful recreation of Shakespeare's 'lovely fantasy'; there are certain elements of it which foreshadow the 'darker dreams' of Peter Brook and Peter Hall. Any oppositional or contradictory elements within the play are however firmly integrated into a cohesive totality analogous to the harmony of music:

> The discord becomes musical ... All of this repetition and counterpoint is, of course, reinforced by Mendelssohn's music, in which themes and styles associated with the plot ... are subtly varied and blended in a harmonious whole. (Jorgens, *Shakespeare on Film*, p. 40).

Shakespeare's play, as Theseus's speech on reason alone will sufficiently indicate, depends for its significant structure on the establishing of contradictions. If there is no sense of *difference* between city and forest, court and carpenter's shop, between the Dionysiac irrationality of emotion and fantasy and the Apollonian rigidity of intellect and law, then the play's contents will flow and blend into a monotonous neutrality – either Theseus's dimension of 'cool reason' or the alternative realm of 'antique fable'. It is up to the director (as it is up to the critical reader) to interpret the structure of these contradictions: the play can with equal legitimacy be seen as a resolution of discords, or as an interweaving of contraries which are left precariously balanced and essentially unresolved in the conclusion. If the drama is produced as pure fantasy, with no sense of difference, then clearly the interpretation will automatically commit itself to the first of these possibilities. In Reinhardt's version of *A Midsummer Night's Dream*, the seamless unity of a perfected work of art transcends the irreducible complexities of 'stark reality' and offers the spectator nothing more intriguing than a transient and compensatory wish-fulfilment fantasy. As we shall see presently, Reinhard's remarkable handling of the film's conclusion offers some degree of qualification to this general judgement.

Reinhardt's film was aimed at the commercial cinema, and at the mass audience of the 1930s which enjoyed musicals, romantic comedy and farce. Peter Hall's version belongs to a very different cultural context, that of a Royal Shakespeare Company production initially turned into a film for American television. Where Reinhardt openly translated Shakespeare's play into a contemporary medium of popular culture, subordinating the dramatic text to spectacle and music, Hall insisted that the film should be a visual embodiment of the text, fleshing the verbal structure with the concrete experience it signifies, but controlled absolutely by the authoritative structure and rhythm of the text. This conception of how a Shakespeare play should be filmed was expounded in an interview with Roger Manvell:

The greatest influence on me, or my generation, was Leavis, who believed above everything in a critical examination of the text, the search for meaning and metaphor … Too much normal film art contradicts the techniques of the plays, at least as far as their most important element, the text, is concerned. But the medium of film can certainly be used to communicate the text most effectively, even to the extent of making its meaning clearer than is sometimes possible in the theatre … This is not a film *from* a stage production or a film *based* on the play. It attempts to bend the medium of the film to reveal the full quality of the text. (Manvell, *Shakespeare and the Film*, pp. 121–6)

Hall's approach to film was therefore much more *literary* than Reinhardt's. Reinhardt strove to escape from a literary kind of theatre altogether: Hall wanted to collapse the medium of film back into the text. He even wondered whether perhaps his film of *A Midsummer Night's Dream* was 'not a film at all', but an experiment in forcing the values privileged by that particular (Leavisite) school of literary criticism – muscular verse, concrete imagery, the authentic rhythm of the speaking voice, integrated organic form – into the medium of film.

Hall's film opens with a deliberate disruption of naturalist film conventions: superimposed on the image of a typical neoclassical 'English country house', surrounded by visual associations of order and authority, appears the title 'Athens'. In place of the more familiar naturalistic techniques of cinema, which would require here an 'establishing shot' to give the spectator a clear idea of 'where' and 'when' we are, this film subverts normal habits of perception by showing us a stereotypical image, and then attaching to it a surprisingly discordant label. The 'Athenian' court is set in a chaste, barren and colourless environment, filmed with a telephoto lens to make the screen image less solid, more two-dimensional.

To take the spectator from court to forest, Hall uses further disruptive devices such as 'jump-cuts', letting the narrative rhythm of the text produce a cinematic technique of *montage*.

The forest sequences were shot with a hand-held camera so that the spectator is aware, from the slightly irregular movements of the frame, of the camera as a recorder of this simulated 'reality'. The actors frequently address the camera directly, demolishing the 'fourth wall' convention of naturalism. The magic of Oberon is emulated by conjuring tricks of cinematography, as Puck appears and disappears, and the disjunctive editing confuses all regular sense of time and space. Puck's concluding invitation to the audience to:

> Think but this, and all is mended:
> That you have but slumbered here
> Whilst these visions did appear.
> And this weak and idle theme,
> No more yielding but a dream.
>
> (V.1.414–418)

is spoken in darkness. Puck snaps his fingers, and it is morning. Which is the reality, which the illusion: daylight and the solid facade of Theseus's rationalistic Athens, or the 'magic' of the forest, as rendered by the film's playful and defamiliarising cinematography?

In many ways Hall's version of *A Midsummer Night's Dream* produces from a filmic imitation of the text an experimental, avant-garde form of cinema which is highly successful in representing the play's ambivalent exploration of the shifting, elusive relations between reality and illusion. It is precisely because literature and film are such different forms of narrative and representation, that the attempt to make one imitate the other precisely resulted in a radically new method of screening Shakespeare.

Hall also, however, followed Leavis's critical method in his general interpretation of the play's closure, and in this respect the film works to close up, in a move towards ideological reconciliation, what its avant-garde cinematography has opened. From Leavis, Hall learned that a successful work of art is one in which inner contradictions are perfectly balanced and reconciled, in a formal structure which mirrors the moral stability of the author. When Hall's 'mechanicals' present their play, the courtly audience is thoroughly involved in a shared experience of festive celebration. Hall cheated on his respect for the text by cutting some of the courtiers' condescending comments, and dramatised a scene in which the lovers seem to have benefited from their flirtation with the occult thus enabling them to take their places in a society united into community by the combined magic of supernatural agency and enthusiastic popular theatricals.

In this respect Hall's film provides a curious contrast with Reinhardt's. When Reinhardt's 'mechanicals' return to perform their burgomask dance to the Athenian court, they find the courtiers gone, having forgotten all about them thus leaving the amateur actors playing to an empty house. This detail may be little more than a director's nightmare but it is enough to cast a shadow, very much in the spirit of Shakespearean comedy, across the play's harmonious resolution. So Reinhardt's operatic extravaganza is shadowed by the foregrounding of an unassimilated element, excluded from the strategic alliance of court and forest; while Peter Hall's self-reflexive and radical cinematic experiment is ultimately pulled back towards a resolution expressing a faith in the possibility of community and reconciliation which would be hard to find in Shakespeare's ambivalent dramatic text.

๛

Akira Kurosawa's *Throne of Blood* (1957) is the most complete translation of Shakespeare into film. The text is abandoned altogether, not even translated; the action shifted from medieval Scotland to feudal Japan; a western Renaissance tragedy becomes an Oriental samurai epic. This most celebrated of all Shakespeare films has been praised particularly for the completeness of its transformation of drama into cinema: 'the great masterpiece' (Peter Brook), 'the finest of the Shakespeare movies' (Grigori Kozintsev). Critics have stressed the *independence* of play and film: Frank Kermode called it 'an allusion to *Macbeth*' and Peter

Brook asserted that it 'doesn't come into the Shakespeare question at all'. J. Blumenthal calls it 'a masterpiece in its own right', wholly liberated from 'the dreaded literary media'.[7] Clearly, if play and film occupy entirely different spaces and cannot even be compared, much less evaluated, against one another: not only do the separate 'masterpieces' enjoy their independent prestige, but the film is rendered incapable of violating the integrity of 'Shakespeare', unable to interrogate or subvert the play's immortal and immanent identity. If this proposition were accepted, *Throne of Blood* would disappear from 'the Shakespeare question' altogether and would offer the possibility of meaning only in relation to Kurosawa's other work and to Japanese culture, ideology and society.[8]

The most substantial critical objection made against the film is that it robs Shakespeare's play of its tragic form and style: 'Kurosawa's Macbeth is not grand';[9] 'His crime is not against God but against Society' (Zambrano, *'Throne of Blood'*, p. 269); 'Kurosawa has betrayed the power of the play'.[10] In fact this is clearly a fundamental aesthetic strategy of the film, which begins in a style more epic than tragic, with a chorus commenting on the images of a ruined castle and a grave: 'Behold within this place now desolate stood once a mighty fortress,/Lived a proud warrior murdered by ambition, his spirit walking still./Vain pride, then as now, will lead ambition to the kill.' The film's narrative is thus framed by an artistic device which contains the story in an explicit moral meaning offered for consideration, to an epic rather than a dramatic audience. Epic detachment is also characteristic of the film's visual style, which is largely structured by the conventions of Japanese Noh drama. Acting and *mise-en-scène* are conventionalised rather than naturalistic; 'Noh is ritual drama, and the world of the Noh is both closed and artificial' (Richie, *Films of Akira Kurosawa*, p. 117). The camerawork, as Kurosawa himself declared, entailed a deliberate avoidance of close-ups (*ibid.*, p.121). The effect of this technique is detachment: 'the camera and chorus maintain an aesthetic distance from the action' (Zambrano, 'Throne of Blood', p.16); or as Donald Richie terms it, 'alienation': ' … alienation is one of the effects of moving the camera back just as moving it forward suggests empathy. The full-shot reveals everything … it disengages the viewer and allows him to see cause and effect' (Richie, *Films of Akira Kurosawa*, p.121).

What can this cinematic interpretation tell us about Shakespeare's *Macbeth*? To begin with, it locates the problem of regicide (*ge-koku-jo*) into a very specific historical and social context, parallel with Duncan's feudal Scotland but radically unlike Shakespeare's England or the modern world. The film displays a militaristic society with an elaborate code of loyalty, expressed in conventionalised social rituals: the intensely stylised social intercourse of samurai and lord seeks to control the power and violence by which such a society exists. 'Ambition' in this society is not some eccentric personality disorder, but a central historical contradiction: a natural extension of the militaristic violence which is both liberated and restrained by the feudal pattern of authority. 'What samurai does not want to be lord of the castle?' Washizu (Macbeth) asks Miki (Banquo). The question cannot be explained away in psychological terms, nor collapsed into a universalist moral system. It has meaning only within the historical world of film. To adopt a similar perspective on *Macbeth* would entail a focus on the play's reconstruction of a distant society, observed not as a shadowy presage of the present, nor as a universal, providentially established natural kingdom of the past. *Macbeth* opens with a startling contradiction: between the ugly, violent butchery described by the captain, in his account of Macbeth's killing of Macdonald; and the elaborate rhetoric of chivalry and courtesy used by Duncan to control that power. Macbeth is bound to Duncan by that language of trust, loyalty, honour but also by a social relationship which depends on a vulnerable and unstable division of authority and power. When Duncan declares Malcolm his successor (a declaration which indicates that this is *not* a hereditary dynasty) he is simultaneously creating a hierarchy and rendering it open to assault by suppressing the very power, vested in the thanes, which sustains his authority.

Critics have complained about the film's understanding of tragic 'inevitability' as social rather than psychological or supernatural: 'Washizu is given social and biological excuses for what can only be put down to unfathomable greed in Shakespeare's Macbeth' (Gerlach, 'Shakespeare, Kurosawa and *Macbeth*', p. 357). But it is evident that *both* Kurosawa's film *and* Shakespeare's play can be seen primarily as *social* tragedies, set within a distanced historical context in which social problems and contradictions can be rendered visible and fully intelligible to the audience's *curiosity*. Furthermore, tragedy narrated with such aesthetic detachment becomes 'epic'. The *tragedy* of Macbeth involves some degree of empathetic involvement by the spectator in the protagonist's experience; like Malcolm, we identify with Macbeth in order to live imaginatively through the knowledge of evil in a cathartic purgation. *Throne of Blood* denies the spectator that experience, and offers in its place, in the epic style, a detached scrutiny of certain actions and events within a certain social context. The choreographed artifice of Noh drama can certainly express a sense of constraint and predetermined destiny but the artifice is invisible, self-evident and self-conscious; the actors are acting out a stylised performance, not miming an inevitable process of psychological development. Again, it is valid to see *Macbeth* itself as an epic rather than a tragic drama. A performance of the play in Elizabethan stage conditions would have possessed certain qualities evident in the film (excluding of course the film's location sequences): bare sets, conventionalised acting, certain possibilities for detachment and alienation (consider Macbeth's self-reflexive characterisation of himself as a 'poor player'), and the acting-out of a well-known story the outcome of which is known beforehand. Even the soliloquies, so highly privileged by modern psychological interpretations, would not have been played as intense self-communings but as colloquies, dialogues between actor and audience. This is no mere academic speculation: Trevor Nunn's 1976 television production of *Macbeth* brings out these qualities of the play with startling distinctness: using a bare studio, actors visible *as* actors, nondescript costume, direct addresses to camera; all techniques which foreground the 'epic' rather than the 'tragic' dimensions of the play.

I am not attempting to argue that Kurosawa has discovered and expressed the *true meaning* of Shakespeare's play: that would be to acknowledge that the text has an authentic, immanent meaning released by a particular act of interpretation. *Throne of Blood* is self-evidently *not* Shakespeare; and therein lies its incomparable value for strategic use in a radical exploration of the play. If the text can be reproduced in a virtually unrecognisable form, then the plurality of the text is proved beyond reasonable doubt. This bastard offspring, the play's *alter ego*, can then be brought back into conjunction with the text, to liberate some of its more radical possibilities of meaning.

Shakespeare Rewound (1993)

꙳

T HIS CHAPTER proposes to argue that certain relatively little-known screen adaptations[1] of Shakespeare's plays can be shown to exemplify and embody constructive explorations of certain key issues widely recognised as central to the problems of contemporary Shakespeare interpretation. The film-texts in question are marginal to the point of invisibility, either because of their institutional origin and technological medium, or because normative criticism has yet to find a means of reconciling their 'alternative' character with the apparatus of critical analysis and interpretation. The formative context of this argument is shaped by the conviction that there now exists a canonical apparatus of 'Shakespeare on film', authorised by a legitimating body of criticism and scholarship.

The 'Shakespeare-on-film' canon could already be seen in the process of construction in those critical studies which still at present constitute the standard literature in the field: the late Roger Manvell's *Shakespeare and the Film* (1971, revised 1979), Charles Eckert's edited collection *Focus on Shakespearean Films* (1972) and Jack Jorgens's *Shakespeare on Film* (1977).[2] Groundbreaking, pioneering, vitally necessary and perennially useful studies, these books together conspire to privilege a particular canon of great films of great plays by great directors – Olivier,

Welles, Kozintsev, Kurosawa, Brook – with a supporting team of somewhat lesser but notable directors in Reinhardt, Mankiewicz, Zeffirelli, Polanski, and a substitute bench of praiseworthy parvenues such as Tony Richardson, Peter Hall, Stuart Burge and Renato Castellani. The methodology of such canonical appropriation entails three principal strategies. One is the assumption that there were no genuinely filmic adaptations of Shakespeare before the invention of sound technology.[3] The second is an 'auteur' theory of film production, which permits the authorising signature of the 'great' (invariably male) director to act as proxy for the 'great' (irrefutably male) dramatist. The third is a positioning of all discussion on the matrix of a putative relation, or system of relations, between the film and some conception of 'the Shakespeare text'.

The body of normative criticism helping to hold this structure in place was augmented by Anthony Davies's *Filming Shakespeare's Plays*,[4] which consolidated in fine style what was already clearly visible as the Great Tradition of Shakespeare-on-film. This book studies the work of four great directors (Olivier, Welles, Brook, Kurosawa), and their great films of the four great tragedies (plus Welles's virtually-tragic *Chimes at Midnight*, and that exception to all rules, Olivier's non-tragic but inexplicably great *Henry V*). Davies confidently affirms, in the closing words of the book, that his subject is the work of 'the world's greatest dramatist'; and his selective focus closes the circle of greatness in a hermetically sealed ellipsis firmly excluding alternative possibilities which might challenge the basis of the structural totality.

Davies draws his theoretical problematic from André Bazin, distinguishing between theatre and cinema, live performance and film, in terms of a hierarchised configuration of cultural levels. A theatre audience can be assumed to possess a certain degree of cultural competence, so that a staged version of a classic play is received as one version among several of a familiar original. A cinema audience is more prone to accept (as in Bazin's theory) what it sees at face value, and thus to mistake the simulacrum of a filmic interpretation for the original itself: cinema spectators are 'less able to set a particular presentation of a play in context' (Davies, p. 3). In the case of filmed Shakespeare, the cinema runs the risk of undermining and supplanting the 'original' by presenting the spectator with an apparently independent 'fixed text'.

The model of relationship between text and film adaptation at work in this study is hierarchical and élitist in its cultural politics. Topping the hierarchy are the Shakespeare texts 'themselves'. In the theatre, dramatic adaptation takes place in a context of informed cultural competence, so that the level of collateral damage to the cultural hierarchy is minimised. In the cinema and on television, the plays enter a dimension of potential contamination by exposure to the limited intelligibility threshold of the average spectator, who is likely to confuse Roman Polanski's *Macbeth* with Shakespeare's 'true originall copie'. Davies approaches each film adaptation as a more or less responsible translation into an appropriately cinematic language of one of a limited range of permissible interpretations of Shakespeare's original play. The director's control over the film's 'vision' is assumed to be absolute. If that directorial authority can be shown as weak or insecure (as in the case of Welles's *Macbeth*), then the film becomes disunified, incoherent, an artistic failure. The job of the critic within this theoretical apparatus is a straightforward one: it is the duty of painstaking formal analysis devoted to interpretation of the film-texts, in relation to the fixed parameters of the Shakespearean text, the aesthetic and technical character of cinema, and the directorial vision.

I am not arguing that Davies's book is not a good and useful study;[5] only that it provides symptomatic evidence that there is now firmly established a 'Shakespeare-on-film' canon which can be used to underpin the authority of a hegemonic critical discourse. If such a cultural apparatus does exist, then the work of deconstructing it must also begin. Here I want to essay a general reconsideration, provisionally sustained by the specific examples discussed here, of that basic theoretical problem, the relation between film and 'Shakespearean text'.

It should be evident by now that the 'Shakespeare-on-film' apparatus has the power to produce its own notion of Shakespearean textuality, which can then be invoked as a validating guarantee of authenticity in adaptation. Here the privileging of the four great tragedies, deriving from a long critical tradition, consolidated at strategic historical points by the Romantic critics, A.C. Bradley and G. Wilson Knight, carries with it the full charge of liberal-humanist values – universality, spiritual liberation and enlightenment through suffering, sacrifice and redemption. To sustain such a universalising capacity, both plays and films need the traditional resources attributed to Shakespeare by post-Romantic criticism – coherent narrative, intelligible character, meaningful action, significant imagery, organic aesthetic form. The critical apparatus of Shakespeare-on-film systematically invokes these criteria in application to the film-texts, thereby reproducing the films as narrative, character, action, imagery, organic form.

The film-texts themselves, drawing as they do on a certain history of film conventions and a certain history of theatre, frequently work to endorse this methodology, shaping their own reconstructions of the Shakespearean theatrical narrative along lines prescribed by contemporary cultural priorities. Olivier's Freudian reading of *Hamlet* produces a film-text that resembles an analyst's report more than it does an imaginative exploration of the unconscious: the introspective character of the Prince, the Expressionist castle, the extravagantly Oedipal gestures, are comprehensively controlled by a unifying narrative which marshals all filmic elements into coherence, order, symmetry – exemplified nowhere better than the shot which positions Hamlet standing over the slain body of Claudius, surrounded by a perfect circle of guards whose extended pikes constellate the victorious revenger as the centre of a ring, the hub of a wheel, the still point of a turning world. The film treatment is hardly, in any truly Freudian sense, the stuff that dreams are made of, and it does not answer readily to the preoccupations of modern psychoanalysis.

Kozintsev's Marxist reading of *King Lear* discomposed the Shakespearean theatrical narrative only in order to produce what is basically a Romantic, almost nineteenth-century narrative of exploitation, poverty, endurance, spiritual discovery. Lear's lunatic ravings about the inequalities of rich and poor become in the Soviet treatment gentle, irrefutably rational statements of self-evident fact. The cyclical collapses of society into ruin and disaster are balanced by the foregrounding of a romantic narrative in which Edgar falls only to rise as the hero of an epic human resistance. Even Peter Brook's *Lear*, acknowledged by many critics for its liberty of adaptation, its avant-garde techniques and its repudiation of ideological consolations, substitutes for a putative narrative of sacrifice and redemption another narrative, still coherent even in its affirmations of incoherence, yet rational in its revelations of unreason. Even those films that push the formal dissonances of this narrative medium to extreme limits – Welles's *Othello*, Brook's *Lear*, Kurosawa's *Throne of Blood* – are operating within parameters prescribed by an authoritative critical apparatus, by the hegemonic sway of realism over the medium of cinema, and by the dominance of naturalism in the theatre.

Returning from these grand, coherent tragic narratives (in which meaningful actions are performed by intelligible characters within the significant imagery of an organic aesthetic form) to 'the Shakespeare text' as we encounter it in the 1990s, we find a significant displacement. Contemporary criticism can no longer provide us with any support for the concept of a stable, coherent text on the basis of which such exercises in filmic textualisation could effectively be accomplished. The modern Shakespeare text is, in virtually all its critical and scholarly manifestations, remarkably unstable, self-contradictory, fissured, labile, permeated by a radical indecideability. For deconstruction, the text's ostensible coherence is there to be systematically discompounded. For Marxist and cultural-materialist criticism, the ideology of the text is there to be rubbed against the grain, demystified and exposed. For feminism the text's patriarchal inflections are there to be combated by an overtly ideological re-reading. For New Historicism the text's spurious individuality is to be challenged by its absorption into a general context of discursive practice. For psychoanalytic approaches the latent sub-text will reveal more meaning than the mechanism of repression that is its surface meaning. For post-modern readings the text is alive only in so far as it resists ideological closure and metanarrative authority, making its resources available for irresponsible play. For theatre studies the text appears in so many radically incompatible manifestations in different stage productions that any notion of a central coherence begins to look like a convenient fiction. For film studies traditional literary-critical methods may well seem to produce a fictitious coherence belied by a method of reading which focuses on specifically filmic language such as film narrative and editing. For textual bibliography, the 'plays' traditionally stabilised in idealised compilation texts are splitting apart into variant and equally valid textualisations.

What would be the nature of a filmed Shakespeare which answered to these contemporary definitions of Shakespearean textuality, as an alternative to that Great Tradition of 'Shakespeare-on-Film' which sustains outmoded nineteenth- and twentieth-century models of narrative, character, action, imagery and form? One answer is to point to a particular tradition of 'underground' film adaptations which seems to me to deserve far more attention (and celebration) than has hitherto been the case, and which seems to me capable of bearing some of these interpretative responsibilities. Another answer would be to contemplate various avenues of lost possibility in the intertwined histories of theatre, film and Shakespearean adaptation. John Collick in *Shakespeare, Cinema and Society*[6] has traced certain historical inter-relations between developments in the nineteenth-century theatre (such as the substitution for verbal drama of a visual and musical language of theatre, enforced by the

Patent Laws) and the origins of silent film (Collick, pp. 33-57). From this configuration arose the Symbolist theatre of Appia and Craig, in which the elements of visual design and music grew correspondingly in importance relative to the authority of the verbal text. Such a theatre is predisposed towards the deconstruction of dramatic literature and interpretative traditions that are fundamentally rooted in verbal language. As is also, in a different way, the theatre of Antonin Artaud,[7] with its revolutionary demand for a new language of theatre, replacing verbal narrative and dialogue with physical gesture and interaction, visual design, non-verbal vocalisation. Both the 'theatre of light' fostered by Appia and Craig, and Artaud's 'theatre of cruelty' are resistant to conventional notions of character, to linear narrative, to the logocentric authority of a world controlled and ordered by and in written or spoken language.

Theatrical work inspired by these models is necessarily avant-garde and deconstructionist in relation to canonical authority and textual authenticity – Charles Marowitz's collage versions of Shakespeare for instance exemplify the influence of Artaud.[8] For examples of filmed Shakespeare based on theatrical influences of this type we need to look beyond the confines of the Great Tradition of Shakespeare-on-film. It is equally important however to recognise that the art of film, so widely and routinely employed as a medium of naturalistic representation, has become so only as a consequence of specific cultural and institutional applications of the technology; and that in its infancy film art manifested itself as a means of creating illusion, as well as a means of representing reality. The experimental cinema of George Melies, like the Symbolist theatre of Appia and Craig and the physical theatre-language of Artaud, offered a genuine though eventually defeated alternative, surfacing later in the Surrealist cinema of Luis Brunuel and Jean-Luc Godard, to the ultimate victory of naturalism in film. Here the grotesque and irrational symbolism of Freudian 'dreamwork' is presented directly, without normative mediation, to the spectator. Melies, as John Collick has observed, 'continually set out to destroy the orthodox logic of narrative-based drama. Instead he built a multitude of strictly enclosed images that, like dreams or hallucinations, possessed their own transgressive rationale' (Collick, p. 74).

There are then within the histories of theatre and film, as well as within the methodologies of contemporary post-structuralist criticism, resources for the production of an alternative 'Shakespeare-on-film'. I will now turn to some brief descriptive analyses of several adaptations exemplifying this underground movement in practice. Since some of my examples, being productions of *Hamlet*, do not, in terms of content, escape from the territory of the Great Tradition, I will, by way of a preliminary positioning, glance at some antecedents from Craig and Melies, tracing a continuity to Coronado and the Cambridge Experimental Theatre. I will close with a discussion of Derek Jarman's *The Tempest* which should, in my view, have already put this kind of Shakespeare cinema on both the cultural map and the theoretical agenda.

In 1912 Edward Gordon Craig was invited to Russia to work with Stanislavsky on the Moscow Art Theatre's production of *Hamlet*. The history of this production, which was not in anyone's view a success, is that of a struggle between competing and incompatible theoretical approaches to drama, particularly those of Stanislavsky and Craig. Craig, who believed the theatre was choked with words, wanted to replace them wherever possible by the visual eloquence of design, *mise-en-scène*, gesture and music. In the MAT *Hamlet* Craig tried to eliminate the boundaries between all the various aspects of the performance: plot, characterisation, scenery and lighting. Linear narrative should be subdued to the synchronic Expressionism of spectacle and design; character too became of minimal importance, with the actors conceived as 'marionettes' to be manipulated within the designer's plan. One of Craig's bright ideas, firmly rejected by Stanislavsky, but documented in one of Craig's production sketches, was that the figure of Hamlet should at all times be accompanied by a companion figure, a 'Daemon death' symbolising the protagonist's relationship with fate. Craig described having dreamed of a 'bright golden figure' who approaches Hamlet during his 'To be or not to be' soliloquy, and thereafter never leaves his side. In keeping with Expressionist methods, the divided inner consciousness of the hero, normally contained within the dramatic speech and within the brooding introspection of the character, is extrapolated into exterior symbolism.[9]

To a literary-critical reading such an idea will appear extravagantly unnecessary. To certain kinds of theatrical approach (though not Stanislavsky's) it may seem a possible avenue of exploration. For a film-maker willing to experiment with Expressionist, Symbolist or Surrealist techniques, who is confronted with a classic dramatic moment (such as Hamlet's famous soliloquy) that is obdurately fixed in the non-visual media of verbal dialogue and interiorised thought, such a possibility could well appear as a breakthrough. George Melies had already in 1907 made his one-reel fantasy of *Hamlet*, in which the entire action becomes a series of encounters between a demented Hamlet and various 'apparitions'. The other characters of the play are transformed into hallucinatory presences which assail Hamlet, but are represented in the film's fantasy medium as external to the Prince's mind.

> He attempts to grasp them in vain, and he falls to brooding. Now is shown the scene in which he meets the Ghost of his father and is told to take vengeance on the reigning monarch, his uncle; but not content with this, Hamlet's fate tantalises him further by sending into his presence the ghost of his departed sweetheart, Ophelia. He attempts to embrace her as she throws flowers to him from a garland on her brow, but his efforts are futile; and when he sees the apparition fall to the ground he, too, swoons away, and is thus found by several courtiers.[10]

The 'apparition' of Ophelia in Melies's film is clearly related to the 'daemon death' of Craig's *Hamlet* design. In each case a theatrical or filmic medium of an Expressionist, Symbolist or Surrealist kind is able to dispense with both narrative and character as traditionally understood, and to operate on an aesthetic plane where the binary oppositions between truth and reality, interior and exterior, reality and fantasy begin to break down. In Celestino Coronado's *Hamlet* (1979) this device of visual doubling is taken much further. The film opens with a whispered voice-over rendering of some lines from the 'To be or not to be' soliloquy, accompanied by intermittently flashing, distorted images. There is a strange noise of wind without any visual climatic accompaniment (there is no castle, no battlements). A miniature figure momentarily appears, naked and crucified, to the accompaniment of an Artaudian 'primal scream'. Hamlet lies on a bed which could be an operating table, or a slab in a morgue, partially covered by a sheet. His face, pointed towards the camera, is inverted, so that a tight close-up shot frames grotesquely distorted features. The miniature figure again appears, montaged over Hamlet's face, again punctuated by the Artaudian scream. The Ghost then appears at the head of the bed, Hamlet's face propped at an angle towards the camera, the body grotesquely foreshortened. The Ghost is naked, standing in a posture of crucifixion, pain and anger expressed graphically through visible muscular tension. The figure that initially appeared as a figment of imagination, a mote to trouble the mind's eye, now stands fully incarnated beside Hamlet. And the two figures are virtually identical.

The Ghost and Hamlet in this film are played by twins, Anthony and David Meyer. The reassuring binary oppositions which conventionally divide the living from the dead, father and son, real presence and imaginary fantasy, immediately break down. In this opening scene the Ghost has his natural colour, while the face of the living prince is by a stark reversal chalky white. As the Ghost delivers his temptation, his face leans towards Hamlet until their lips virtually touch: the Ghost's searing communication is breathed, inspired directly into the Prince's passive and receptive body, and the faces form a mirror-image, a disconcerting doubleness that confuses the dividing line between self and other. In the 'nunnery' scene, as Hamlet speaks with Ophelia, the Ghost stands behind him, then leaps onto him and from behind grapples his throat. The vocal line passes from the gentle Prince to the ferocious and vindictive Ghost, who finally pushes Hamlet aside to become the Prince himself. The physical combat is re-enacted in the final scene when the twins interchangeably play Hamlet and Laertes.

Gertrude and Ophelia are also played by the same actress, Helen Mirren, a doubling which presents some intriguing displacements in the female roles. Ophelia is played as a 'dumb blonde', erotically passive and slow of wit. Gertrude is played as a mature and powerful woman, confident in her overt sensuality. But the two can pass into one another and exchange identities. In the nunnery scene already described, the Hamlet/Ghost figure uses a red grease paint stick (which is both phallic and cosmetic, erotic and violent) to inscribe marks of violation on Ophelia's throat (compare 'I will speak daggers to her, but use none'). This is simultaneously Hamlet taking his revenge on Ophelia as woman, and the Ghost wreaking a fevered sensual assault on Gertrude his treacherous wife. At first Ophelia/Gertrude swoons in helpless sensual passivity as the male figure vents on her body his lust and anger. Then, in a startling reversal, she recovers her poise and emerges from the 'status-game' having defeated the Ghost/Hamlet (who in turn falls helplessly away) with a smile of frank sensual power.

Coronado's *Hamlet* escapes attention in all the critical literature on the subject of Shakespeare-on-film (though his subsequent 1984 production of *A Midsummer Night's Dream* in collaboration with Lindsay Kemp is discussed by Collick (pp. 103–5). *Hamlet* was produced in 1979 at the Royal College of Art, London, by professional actors working with staff and students of the Department of Design, North London Polytechnic. The contingent institutional context was thus one of public sector higher education. The informing theatrical context was that of small-scale, avant-garde experimental theatre, with a clear theoretical link to Artaud, a visual context familiar with Surrealism and the 'theatre of light', and a background in the kind of intensive improvisation and experiment appropriate rather to the studio of a drama school or a theatre department than to a film studio.

Patently low budget, studio-based, even in some ways amateurish, this film seems to me quite extraordinarily resourceful in the inventive openness of its explorations into possible relations between text and performance. Here we have a film treatment attuned to the intellectual sophistication and imaginative complexity of the post-structuralist, post-modern Shakespeare text. When Hamlet delivers the 'too, too sullied flesh' soliloquy, the camera dissolves his face into a cubist montage of diverging faces: the too, too sullied flesh is literally seen melting, as it does in no other film production of *Hamlet*. Ophelia's drowning is a disturbing collage of dismembered features – ears, nose, eyes, teeth and tongue – glimpsed under water, poetically split and separated as they so often are in the fetishistic poetry of the play. When Hamlet in the 'closet scene' urges his mother to 'look but upon this picture', what they see is the grotesque, corpulent body of Claudius, hammering one bloodstained hand repeatedly onto a cluster of nails. Is the image a wish-fulfilment fantasy of Hamlet's? Gertrude's perverse fantasy of sexual gratification through violence? Or a representation of the King, tortured by remorse into self-mutilation? The experimental medium of the film allows all these possibilities of meaning, together with many others, to circulate abundantly through the spectator's consciousness in a condition of radical indecideability very close to deconstruction.

In 1987 the Audio-Visual Unit of Cambridgeshire College of Arts and Technology (now Anglia Polytechnic University) produced a videotape version of another avant-garde, studio adaptation of *Hamlet* performed by Cambridge Experimental Theatre. Roland Kenyon's deconstructive reworking of *Hamlet* is staged in an empty studio by a small ensemble of two men and two women. There are no props, not even a skull. The 'text' is cut, transposed and re-aligned with a Marowitzean disregard for the principles of textual integrity, classical narrative and inferred authorial intention. The production is, for a start, a *Hamlet* without the Prince of Denmark: the four actors are cast as Gertrude, Claudius, Ophelia and Polonius, and the lines of the dispossessed prince are re-distributed between them. The great individuated hero of Romantic tradition is abolished at a stroke, and with him disappear all the modern bourgeois myths of subjectivity. 'Character' is fractured, fragmented, dissipated and re-born as dramatic interaction and social interdependence.

In support of these explorations Cambridge Experimental Theatre invoked post-structuralist theory, the psychology of personality and the nature of 'subjectivity' in Renaissance culture. In the performance, individuality is minimalised by neutral uniformity of costume, mask-like face-painting and the simultaneous fragmenting and re-orchestration of the verbal text – collective choric delivery, broken and interrupted cadences, emotional tones rubbing against the grain of patent sense-meaning. And although the production displays an emphatic and particularising concern with verbal communication (akin, as I suggest below, to some of the more formalistic techniques of language analysis employed in deconstructionist criticism) its primary medium is physical: an attempt at devising an eloquence of the body, of visual gesture constructing significant compositions of physical space.

The filming of this production was by no means a straightforward transmission of stage performance to screen. Interacting with the avant-garde techniques of performance employed in the production are a range of deconstructive devices available to the medium of video – freeze-frame, dissolve, silhouette, montage, multi-layered sound and vision mixing. The Shakespearean text is deconstructed twice over, in the course of its passage through stage and onto screen. The video is designed specifically for educational use – it is supplied with a supplementary 'guide', containing both explanatory discussions and practical exercises – and in these terms it has certain advantages over the various feature films, TV productions and other available material. It can be used to challenge traditional notions and to provoke debate about some central issues of both text and performance. Aligned with the received play-text, it can broach a number of contentious issues relating to the passage of text into performance: the sacrosanctity of text, the limits of adaptation, the relative autonomy of performance, the signifying potentialities of verbal communication and physical gesture. Its defamiliarising approach to the most familiar of plays can be used to interrogate deeply rooted assumptions about naturalism, character, narrative. And as an instance of exploratory and creative rapprochement between separate media, it can be used to foreground and call into question not only traditional representations of Shakespeare on the screen, but the nature of filmic representation itself.

It was clearly part of the producers' intentions that the project should be something more than metadrama: that it should accomplish a strategic cultural intervention, should do more than foreground its own deconstructive devices. Nigel Wheale in the supplementary 'guide' links the methodology of the performance to the originating conditions of *Hamlet's* production:

> the Renaissance audience was less interested in the deep ('fully rounded') characterisation of individual roles, but rather would have attended more to the impersonal and communal issues being debated within the drama: questions focusing on the nature of monarchy, the function of religious institutions and belief, and particularly on questions concerning the organisation and conduct of the family. These were controversies centering on personal conduct and property rights which were very pressing in the early modern period. This is to argue that Renaissance drama was overtly didactic in ways which are no longer directly obvious to us. The Cambridge Experimental Theatre production, through its

formalising of verse, action and staging, through the role-sharing, and the intervention of video effects, actively impersonalises the issues of the drama.[11]

In practice the production does not quite do this. Earlier examples of avant-garde 'deconstructive' productions of *Hamlet*, such as Charles Marowitz's collage, or the Coronado film (not sufficiently recognised here as a precedent) were much more interpretative, polemical, and in the broadest sense political, than this one: much more disposed to provoke and precipitate contestation and debate about 'issues' – power, individualism, gender, sexuality. Both these latter adaptations worked against conventional concepts and techniques of representation: but both also managed simultaneously to hew new meanings from the play and to throw it into meaningful juxtaposition with contemporary issues and problems. The methods of Cambridge Experimental Theatre's production are rather those of the more formalistic tendencies of deconstruction: concentrating attention exclusively on the signifying practices of language (whether word or image). It was, for instance, intended that the fragmentation of the role of Hamlet and its dispersal across gender differences would lead to an interrogation of sexual politics in both play and contemporary context (see *Hamlet: A Guide*, pp. 8-9). Yet the rendering uniform by costume and make-up of the actors, and the emphasis on stylised gesture and movement, effectively neutralises gender as it destroys individuality: sexual difference is suppressed rather than subverted.

Derek Jarman's version of *The Tempest* (1980) shows the underground spring of alternative-Shakespeare-on-film temporarily surfacing in the form of art-house cinema. Like Coronado's balletic adaptation of *A Midsummer Night's Dream* (1984), Jarman's film did not go on general release but occupied the minority space of the London avant-garde. *The Tempest* was subsequently broadcast on Channel 4 television. The experimental quality of Jarman's film resides far less in the dimension of technology than the examples so far discussed, despite the fact that in general his films are technically very adventurous. The deconstructionist effects of *The Tempest* operate rather at the levels of textual adaptation and dramatic interpretation: casting, setting, *mise-en-scène*, costume: and sexual politics.

As in Coronado's *Hamlet*, the Shakespearean text (of which there is, like *The Tempest*, only one version, that of 1623) is very freely adapted and cut, with roughly one third of it employed in the film, and with the text that remains often radically transposed and reorganised. Some transpositions force the poetry to operate differently in an altered context. Benedictory lines from the Masque in Act 4 are spoken early in the film by Ariel to Miranda, from his position on the child-woman's rocking horse. The peculiar intimacy, sexless yet erotically playful, created here between the naïve girl and the restless, cynical yet affectionate spirit/slave, marks a clear contrast with the formal betrothal ceremony from which Shakespeare's lines were drawn. Tenderness in this film occurs between alienated individuals, not in the collective social rituals which endorse sexual 'normality'. The speech from the play-text in which Prospero renounces his necromantic power closes on 'by my so potent art', with Prospero gazing into the magic glass through which he is able to see the courtiers held in his enchantment. This Prospero has no intention of giving up his art or his power. Often the dramatic verse operates in the film, in the manner of the 'theatre of light', as a commentary on the visual spectacle, rather than as a substantive means of advancing narrative or developing character; the poetry is, in a sense, 'set to vision' as words can be set to music.

Jarman's principal thematic interests lie in the conception of Prospero as a magician, and in the nature of the 'island' world dramatised by the play, with its strange mixed company of inhabitants. Jarman saw the magic in the play not as a symbol for something else (Christian benevolence or political despotism) but substantively as a form of knowledge, a science. Jarman was certainly more inclined than most to take the occult seriously; but his concern in the film is rather with the kind of exploratory and experimental humane science that magic was in the Renaissance. His earlier film *Jubilee*, a synoptic comparison of the ages of two Queen Elizabeths, features John Dee as a central figure in Renaissance humanism, whose philosophical 'magic' offered a synthesis of science and art. Jarman contrasted this spirit of liberal enquiry, characteristic of the Elizabethan age and of the period of his own formative development (the 1960s and 1970s) with the oppressive view of the occult characteristic of James I, and with the political, cultural and sexual repression of the 1980s. Heathcote Williams, who plays Prospero in the film, is not an actor but an occultist, a writer and magician who (evidently) believes himself to be possessed of necromantic powers. He is also a strikingly young Prospero (the character is generally assumed by tradition to be at least as old as Michael Hordern appears always to have been), so the powers he exercises seem to have little to do with either patriarchal authority or avuncular benevolence. Through the obsessive studies, in which he is engaged for most of the film, are expressed energies of restless physical quickness, an unappeasable curiosity, an enormous hungry vitality and a craving moral appetite to make the world a better place. The treachery, rebelliousness, opposition he encounters at every point seem to him petty irritations obstructing a project of general improvement, rather than deeply wounding personal grievances. There is room in the film, of course, to question Prospero's régime – Caliban, Ariel, Ferdinand are there to focus such interrogation – but in terms of the film's general interpretation, the presentation of Prospero is a positive celebration of the liberal intellectual struggling against a climate of ignorance and repression. The medium of surrealist or fantasy film can also be held, as it has from George Melies onwards, to be a kind of magic capable of attaining through estrangement a new and different knowledge of the world.

> Jarman is a product of the freedom and spirit of enquiry which characterised the English cultural scene in the 1960s and 1970s. His film – and his representation of magic as an intellectual and

imaginative faculty of the utmost significance – is a stand against the puritanism and conservatism which have developed here in the last decade.[12]

It is of course arguable that Jarman has side-stepped the very issues of power and authority that preoccupy modern discussions of this play. But his *Tempest* is no longer a treatment of colonialism. In the film neither Prospero's own domestic empire, nor the courtly community of Milan and Naples, can be held to represent any normative social collectivity. There is very little concrete sense of a 'real world', somewhere else, by reference to which the microcosm of the island could be orientated. The entire population of the island seems literally shipwrecked, utterly alienated from all norms and conventions of social behaviour. Prospero's aspiration seems therefore to be that of bringing an alienated, expatriate community into social cohesion, rather than that of imposing any rules of equity, rights of legitimacy or structures of authority. This effect is achieved partly by the setting of the film, which alternates between an exterior location, shot through a derealising blue filter, on a windswept beach in north-east England; and the dilapidated, Gothic interior of Stoneleigh Abbey, a Tudor mansion in the Midlands, in the half-ruined eighteenth-century wing of which the film's interior sequences are played. The confusion of historical period is exploited through both setting and costume: in rooms of faded Regency splendour, lit only by candles, carpeted by straw and accumulated leaves, characters are dressed in a bizarre mixture of historical costume designs, Prospero in a Romantic style resembling young Werther on one of his most suffering days, while his daughter (the punk singer Toyah Wilcox) bursts the seams of a tight Regency décolleté. Caliban (the blind mime actor Jack Birkett) wears the uniform of a nineteenth-century butler; Ariel the white boiler-suit of a nuclear technician.

These carefully juxtaposed stylistic inconsistencies are exploited to extreme and stunning effect in Jarman's version of the betrothal masque, which in this adaptation closes the film.

Both the courtiers and the co-conspirators of Caliban – who are presented here as farcically comic and quite incredibly ineffectual – are fixed in Prospero's power, and form (in the case of the courtiers) comatose, or (in the case of Caliban, Trinculo and Stephano) enthralled spectators of the entertainment. Jarman replaced the formal masque and attendant ceremonies with a clumsy but good-natured hornpipe executed by extremely camp sailors; followed by the entrance of a single goddess, in the form of cabaret singer Elizabeth Welch, who delivers a delightful 'soul' rendering of 'Stormy Weather'. The entire displaced community of the film – the betrothed couple, who sit on a chaise longue under a shower of confetti; the 'liberated' mariners, who form a swaying, appreciative audience for the singer; Caliban and his co-conspirators, lulled into enraptured submission by the delights of music – are drawn together in a filmic concord which (paradoxically in logic, though perhaps natural in film) depends on the rapprochement of diversity, the yoking together of opposites, the celebration of difference.

'In Shakespeare', wrote Peter Brook in 1968,

> It is through … unreconciled opposition … through an atonal speech of absolutely unsympathetic keys that we get the disturbing and the unforgettable impressions of his plays. It is because the contradictions are so strong that they burn on us so deeply.
>
> Shakespeare's plays were written to be performed continuously … their cinematic structure of alternating short scenes, plot intercut with subplot, were all part of a total shape. This shape is only revealed dynamically, that is, in the uninterrupted sequence of these scenes, and without this their effect and power are lessened as much as would be a film that was projected with breaks and musical interludes between each reel. The Elizabethan stage was … a neutral open platform – just a place with some doors – so it enabled the dramatist effortlessly to whip the spectator through an unlimited succession of illusions … it also allowed him free passage from the world of action to the world of inner impressions.
>
> In an ideal relation with a true actor on a bare stage we would

continually be passing from long shot to close, tracking or jumping in and out – and the planes often overlap. The power of Shakespeare's plays is that they present man simultaneously in all his aspects ... [13]

Here Brook can be seen reading Elizabethan drama cinematically, finding in the technical language of film a modern equivalent for his historical view of how Shakespeare's plays were designed to be performed. He was also, obviously, beginning to think about the problems of filming Shakespearean drama, since his own *King Lear* was in the making by the end of 1968. Brook's insistence here on the need for a 'free passage' from 'the world of action' to 'the world of inner impressions' is one of the bases for the aesthetic shape of that film. It is perhaps equally significant, given the ambitious aesthetic programme expounded here, that *King Lear* does not go further in the direction of an exploration of that theoretical acknowledgement of overdetermination – how to render in cinematic terms, in other words, the 'overlapping planes' of the Shakespeare text. In 1965 Brook proposed that the correct way to gather and grasp these overlapping planes would be to make a film of a Shakespeare play designed to be projected onto three separate screens, each of which would represent a different visual image. Another method is of course that of formal montage, developed in Welles's *Othello*. But perhaps the most successful attempts to capture that elusive, shifting complexity of the Shakespeare text are to be found in the deconstructive experiments of 'underground' cinema. Here at least is a recoverable body of cultural production which seems to offer some degree of filmic equivalent to the modern theoretically activated Shakespearean text.

PART THREE

Case Studies

CHAPTER FIVE

Henry V (1984)

ॐ

CRITICISM – signifying, in a limiting but familiar definition, the formally written academic discourse of literary scholarship, analysis and interpretation – is only one manifestation of the general assemblage of social and ideological practices which operate over the cultural ground we call 'literature'. But it remains, however emphatically we deny its pre-eminence and insist on its relativity, a privileged discourse claiming the status of secondary function to the primary material of 'literature' itself. Writing about literature cannot concern itself only with texts, biographical factors, historical background: it must begin by addressing that history which begins when a piece of writing (or theatre) embarks on its career of consumption by readership or audience: its long history of assimilation into the apparatus of culture, its incorporation into received traditions of the 'canon' of literature, in which context it can be immediately 'recognised'; its implementation into systems and structures of education. Any attempt to define what a literary work 'is' must be preceded by an analysis of what it has become, what certain cultural and educational processes have made of it, and of how and why those operations took place.[1] But can this history be properly termed the history of 'criticism'? Can the science of it be properly defined by Peter Widdowson's coinage 'critiography'?[2] Formal criticism is only a part of the totality of cultural practices: does it remain the dominant, the determinant mode? If so, how and why does it secure and maintain this dominant position?

Recent theoretical work has sought, correctly, to deflect our attention from the empirical analysis of texts, the reconstruction of biographical and historical backgrounds, the sociological investigation of conditions of production; towards a greater concern with the existence of literary texts as they are produced and reproduced in the course of a historical process of cultural, educational, artistic activities of various kinds. Tony Bennett has observed:

> A condition of any text's continuing to exert long-term cultural effects within any society must be that it is constantly brought into connection or articulated with new texts, socially and politically mobilised in different ways within different class practices, differentially inscribed within the practices of educational and linguistic institutions and so on … it is only in the light of such historically concrete, variable and incessantly changing determinations – determinations which so press in upon the text as fundamentally to modify its very mode of being – that it is possible to assess, at any given moment, the effects that might be attributed to any given text or set of texts. [3]

Peter Widdowson has developed this insight into a call for a new kind of 'historical criticism':

> I would propose that if there is to be a 'historical criticism' which is genuinely historical and empirical … it must necessarily involve a conception of critiography. This means a study of texts in history; not merely as productions of their period, nor, then, as receptacles of historical messages from that period which criticism decants, but as cultural productions of the 1980s. This implies, of course, an initial displacement of the apparently neutral 'primary material' from the central focus in favour of the constitutive social discourses which make it available in a determinate form as a present cultural fact. [4]

Widdowson names 'criticism' and 'education' as 'two of the main constitutive discourses' from which 'literature' is constructed;

emphasising that other social determinants such as publication, radio, television and film should also receive attention, since they 'materially affect a text's availability, and, through intertextuality, the ways in which it is read.'

'Shakespeare' is a particularly rich field for this type of investigation, since Shakespeare, conventionally the greatest of English literary figures, has paradoxically been accorded the most widespread and varied extra-literary existence. Readings of Shakespeare which limit themselves to texts, criticism and historical 'background' inevitably begin by implicitly claiming that 'Shakespeare' is immediately accessible as an object of investigation, in the form of immediately readable texts. Certain kinds of critical and pedagogic convention have convinced us that in the act of silent, individual reading of a 'literary' text (the play as 'dramatic poem') we hear directly the voice of the bard, gain immediate access to the thoughts and feelings of his human heart, establish intimate connection with the past in which he wrote. But any attempt to discover the real Shakespeare – whether critical, historical or dramatic – involves peering through a vast and enormously complex system of refracting prisms: the whole multifarious body of ideas, attitudes, assumptions, images, which have accrued over centuries of cultural activity centred on the literary productions of this Elizabethan dramatist, and which constitute at any given historical moment the ideological problematic in which Shakespeare is 'recognised'. Every writer, every mode of writing has this kind of history: in the case of Shakespeare it is not merely the visible history of a literary reputation, but the enormous residuum of centuries of constructing and reconstructing a symbol: a symbol, pre-eminently, of British national culture. 'Shakespeare' is everywhere: not only in criticism, scholarship and historiography, or in the apparatus of education, or in theatrical, television and film productions; but beyond these traditional media of national culture, the phenomenon appears in the fabric of everyday common life, a component of popular culture. It is probable that every English-speaking citizen of Britain has heard of Shakespeare: not necessarily from plays or books, but from tourist attractions, advertisements, television comedies, the names of pubs and beers. In this context 'Shakespeare' (a concept which, we can already see, is partly distinguishable from the writer of plays) appears as a universal symbol of high art, of 'culture', of education, of the English spirit. An agency offering elocution lessons advertised itself by a cartoon of a puzzled Shakespeare bewildered by the voice from a telephone receiver: to be understood by Shakespeare would be a guarantee of correct speaking. In the television series *Batman*, the entrance to the 'Batcave' was controlled by a switch concealed inside a bust of Shakespeare's head: the decorative property of a millionaire's house opens to activate an exotic world of drama and costume, of fantasy and adventure. Immediately we begin to look back at Shakespeare in a historical perspective, it becomes evident that what we see is not Shakespeare in history, but the history of 'Shakespeare'.

A theoretical question very much worth asking is: why is it that, despite the evident *universality* of the Shakespeare phenomenon, formal criticism can still claim to occupy the status of privileged discourse; and is its power and influence as dominant as it so confidently assumes? If a literature like 'Shakespeare' exists self-evidently as a set of social practices, are some of those practices more determinant than others? School pupils all 'read' Shakespeare: they seldom read criticism, except in the form of Study Aids – Coles', Brodie's, and York's Notes. Is their 'Shakespeare' a relatively criticism-free version? Is the Shakespeare who exists in theatrical productions (at all levels from RSC to school play) a more real and influential social fact than the Shakespeare of formal critical discourse? Is the Shakespeare of film and television broadcasts, which play to larger audiences than the plays have ever known, the truly constitutive activity of the present age? What is the relationship between criticism and other forms of cultural reproduction, and how constitutive in fact is it?

The year 1944 represents an interesting focus of Shakespeare

reproduction, and a decisive moment in the ideological reconstruction of the English history plays, especially *Henry V.* 1944
saw the appearance of three texts which represent three different
ideological interventions into the culture of war-time Britain: all
concerned generally with Shakespeare, particularly with the
English history plays, and pre-eminently with *Henry V.* G. Wilson
Knight published a patriotic essay *The Olive and the Sword,* which
had been written in 1940, printed as a pamphlet in 1941, and performed as a play.[5] Laurence Olivier's film of *Henry V,* in the making since 1943, was released. Finally, there appeared the text which
has proved by far the most influential, and which represents a
much more conventional commitment to academic scholarship
and formal criticism: E.M.W. Tillyard's *Shakespeare's History
Plays.*[6] I would like to explore this cultural moment through
analysis of these texts, and suggest some reasons why 'criticism',
however specialised and elitist an activity it may seem to be,
remains the decisively constitutive discourse determining the
nature of 'literature'.

In the 1930s *Scrutiny* (through the work especially of L.C.
Knights)[7] had consolidated 'Shakespeare' the author/work as an
ideological force of cultural and national unity: in the dual form
of a *historical* constituting of Shakespeare as the authentic voice
of an organically homogeneous period of English culture; and a
literary-critical emphasis on textual reading as the only surviving
means available for participating in and reconstructing that lost
totality. *Scrutiny* insisted on the social provenance and social relevance of literature, but nonetheless privileged *criticism* as the only
effective means of gaining access to or recreating that lost harmony of English culture. Both lines of argument were shaped in the
context of a long-running polemic against the simplistic 'econo-
mist' marxism of the 1930s: against that philosophy Leavis,
Knights and others insisted that historical analysis of literature
should be empirical rather than theoretical: and that a primary
element in the study of 'culture' or 'history' should be the critical
'experiencing' of the text.

The social effects of the Second World War placed this ideology under some pressure. The national war effort demanded total participation from every section of society: culture too should apply its powers to the necessary and immediate tasks in hand. *Scrutiny* went its own way, scarcely acknowledging the existence of war. But other kinds of cultural intervention took the call to arms seriously. As both the national poet and a symbol of organic unity in British society, Shakespeare was clearly a candidate for enlistment. The spirit of his 'patriotism' was evoked very early: on 22 February 1939, Neville Chamberlain was quoting from *King John*: 'Come the three corners of the world in arms, And we shall shock them ... '[8]

Wilson Knights' essay represents an early attempt to force literary criticism into the public arena: to break away from *Scrutiny's* concentration on the text and on academic reconstruction, to place the ideological power of 'Shakespeare' at the service of the national war effort. At this point 'Shakespeare', as the visible, concrete embodiment (literature) of a lost social harmony, was brought into direct complicity with that ideology of national unity which the leading sections of British society – government, press and broadcasting media, trades union leadership – were fighting to forge and perpetuate throughout the war. This powerful myth of national unity has been subjected to some interrogation by historians, who have demonstrated some of the mechanisms of its construction, and exposed some of the less heroic realities of war on the Home Front. Angus Calder's book on British society in the Second World War seriously questions the myth of a *People's War*: his evidence and arguments emphasise the discontent as well as the heroism, the persistence of social divisions and conflicts from the 1930s as well as the development of new, more open social relationships. His conclusion is that the war brought no fundamental change in British society:

> Those who made the 'People's War' a slogan argued that the war could promote a revolution in British society. After 1945, it was for a long time fashionable to talk as if something like a revolution

had in fact occurred. But at this distance, we see clearly enough that the effect of the war was not to sweep society on to a new course, but to hasten its progress along the old grooves. [9]

And Henry Pelling's *Britain and the Second World War*[10] confirms this view that the war did not lead to profound social changes.

It is not possible in the scope of this chapter to attempt any serious discussion of this large historical problem: but the problem can be seen as the context in which to describe and evaluate these cultural interventions into a national crisis. If the large-scale social changes which actually *did* take place – the spread of democratic participation in social life, the breaking-down of class barriers, the employment of women, etc. – did not succeed in creating a new society, then considerable powers must be attributed to those political and cultural forces which succeeded in reconstructing British society on the old lines. An examination of the process by which some elements of that myth were constructed may throw some light on the nature of the myth itself.

G. Wilson Knight's essay is as much a piece of wartime propaganda as an essay in literary criticism: if anything, more propaganda than scholarship, since the starting point of the argument is very explicitly not 'literature' but the contemporary situation. His language is not the mannered urbanity of scholarly discourse, but the fierce rhetoric proper to a national crisis: he begins with a direct appeal to the spirit of national unity ('our English heritage') which in his view was forged in 1940 by the imminent threat of invasion, and which he regards as the 'soul of the nation':

> Four years ago [1940] the sudden fusion of parties into a single united British front gave confidence and purpose to a nation in peril. Only when all parties are felt as, in the depths, at one, can the soul of a nation be revealed; as in a human life, when different attributes, body, heart, and mind, pulse together, the soul is known … the soul of England has yet to find, or rather hear, its own voice. (Knight. *Olive and Sword*, p. 1)

The soul of the nation is national unity: in 1940 England found its soul. But the soul has yet to discover its 'true voice'. The true voice of the authentic English soul is apparently to be heard in its literary tradition:

> We have for four years been fighting, alone or in partnership, the reptilian dragon-forces of unregenerate, and therefore unshaped and inhuman instinct, energies breathing fire and slaughter across Europe, because such is our destiny, asserted by our time-honoured national symbol, Saint George, the dragon slayer, whose name our present sovereign bears; and we shall first search out that destiny not in platitudes of half-belief nor any reasonings of our own fabrication, but where alone it rests authentic, in the great heritage we possess of English letters, the greatest accumulation of national prophecy; where the soul of England, which is her essential sovereignty, speaks clearly – in Shakespeare, Milton, Pope, Byron, Blake, Wordsworth, Tennyson, Hardy and many more. (Knight, *Olive and Sword*, p.3)

Because Wilson Knight's ideological strategy here is so explicit, there is little sense of ideological mystification. Clearly 'English literature' is regarded as an object with its own independent mode of existence: it is the true voice of the nation. Yet the idea of the nation's soul 'finding' its voice implies something closer to a conscious and deliberate appropriation and reconstruction of a 'literature' for its usefulness in the contemporary crisis. Knight wishes to assert that literature has spoken of national unity all along, only its utterance has not been heeded. But the urgency of his concern with a pressing present reality suggests strongly that the voice is that of a ventriloquist, with 'Shakespeare' his articulate dummy. The above passage engineers an important slide from the political concept of national unity to the *metaphysical* idea of 'sovereignty'; metaphysical because Knight does not use it as a political term to define the heart of power in a state (in his Britain, constitutionally Parliament) but to allude rather to a spirit of national emotion which manifests itself in the sovereign (the king), but is possessed by the people as a whole. (It would be amusing to consider what some members of Knight's pantheon – Milton, Byron, Blake, Hardy – would have thought of his royalist 'sovereignty').

The greatest expression of this sovereignty, the most authentic expression of England's soul, is Shakespeare:

> If ever a new Messiah is to come, he will come, says the greatest of all American writers, Herman Melville, in the name of Shakespeare. We need expect no Messiah, but we might, at this hour, turn to Shakespeare, a national prophet if ever there was one, concerned deeply with the royal soul of England. That royalty has direct Christian and chivalric affinities. Shakespeare's lifework might be characterised as expanding, through a series of great plays, the one central legend of St. George and the Dragon. Let us face and accept our destiny in the name both of Shakespeare and St. George, the patron saint of our literature and nation. (Knight, *Olive and Sword*, p. 3)

This rhetoric of metaphysical terminology seeks to identify a number of key terms – the nation, the nation's soul, and its voice (literature), the sovereign, Christ, Shakespeare and St. George. The logical absurdity of this argument can easily be exposed; but such exposure does not exhaust its significance, which consists in the directness with which Knight defined the ideological function of literature as he conceived and practised it: 'I aim to show what reserves for the refuelling of national confidence exist in Shakespeare's poetry.' (p.4) Nothing could be clearer than that.

> Shakespeare wrote at a time when, after centuries of civil war, England first became nationally self-conscious … the voice of the new nation is Shakespeare.
>
> His historical plays are mainly studies of internal disorder during the centuries leading to the England of Elizabeth. Shakespeare's thinking functions continuously in terms of order … The issues troubling Europe today are here in embryo; and the desire for world-order which fabricated the League of Nations is an expansion of a desire pulsing through Shakespeare. (Knight, *Olive and Sword*, p.4)

Shakespeare's historical dramas were, for Wilson Knight, parables of 'order' and 'disorder': expressions of an unsentimental patriotism which faces up to the prevalence and the perils of 'disorder', and proudly affirms the potentiality and the imperative necessity of 'order'. Such political terms are used with an apparent innocence of political meaning: what social system constitutes this apparently unquestionable 'order'? In fact Knight's theory is metaphysical rather than political: social order is defined as the English nation united in the symbol of the Crown: 'The Crown symbolises the nation's soul-life, which is also the greater self of each subject.'

This formulation recalls Matthew Arnold's theory of class; we all have a lesser self, which encourages us to consider our own personal interests or the interests of family, faction, social group or class: and a greater self, which urges us to identify with the corporate body of the nation. The form of that identification is the Crown: '... our sole final allegiance is to that whole of which all these are parts and whose symbol is the Crown.'(p. 89) The category of 'order' is thus a substitute for the political definition of a social formation – in this case a bourgeois-democratic state governed by Parliament with an anachronistic figurehead in the form of a vestigial monarchy – and Shakespeare's plays are used to support and confirm an appeal to 'order' which signifies, in effect, a qualified adherence to the *status quo*. The appeal to order is exactly, in fact, that emotion of national unity, which was fostered during the Second World War not just to defeat fascism but to secure the ideological unification of the bitterly divided Britain of the 1930s.

Henry V becomes the focal point of Shakespeare's vision of 'order'. Knight can see no irony, ambiguity or contradiction at all in the play. Henry is 'a Christian warrior, leading, after long periods of civil war, a united nation to foreign conquest'; (p. 29) 'a blend of righteousness with power'; (p. 29) 'a blend of Christian faith and martial heroism'; (p. 32) and the play is 'a new epic and heroic drama, blending Christian virtue with martial prowess'

(p. 29). The over-working of the word 'blend' visible in these quotations is significant: it is one of many such metaphors – 'concord', 'harmony', etc. – displaying the critic's concern to identify the play's formal unity with the unity of England, and both with the desired unity of Britain in 1944. Knight's Henry never puts a foot wrong: even in his masquerade as a common soldier in Act IV, he doesn't commit the error of 'the pernicious socialist doctrine' by levelling himself down to his subjects' status: by their heroism they level themselves up to his royalty. (p. 37)

Wilson Knight's views may seem bizarre – but they have not changed. In June 1982 he said of the Falklands War:

> I have for long accepted the validity of our country's historic contribution, seeing the British Empire as a precursor, or prototype, of world-order. I have relied always on the Shakespearean vision as set forth in my war-time production *This Sceptred Isle* ... Our key throughout is Cranmer's royal prophecy at the conclusion of Shakespeare's last play, *Henry VIII*, Shakespeare's final words to his countrymen. This I still hold to be our one authoritative statement, every word deeply significant, as forecast of the world-order at which we should aim. Though democratic, it involves not just democracy alone, but democracy in strict subservience to the crown as a symbol linking love to power and the social order to the divine ... I tend to support our activities, now or in the future in so far as they may be felt to be expanding British tradition and our national heritage to world proportions, in attunement with Shakespearean prophecy. [11]

The relation of Laurence Olivier's film of *Henry V* to the contemporary war-time situation of its production (1943-4) is as explicit as that of Wilson Knight's jingoistic essay. The film bears an epigraph:

> To the Commandos and Airborne Troops of Great Britain, the spirit of whose ancestors it has been humbly attempted to recapture in some ensuing scenes, this film is dedicated.

Part of the film's intention was clearly identical with that of Wilson Knight's – 'to show what reserves for the refuelling of national confidence exist in Shakespeare's poetry.' Olivier, who was in Hollywood when the war began, learned to fly there in order to join the Fleet Air Arm. In uniform he played the role of patriotic orator to the Home Front: too old for active service, he found opportunities for contributing to the war effort in the form of ideological and cultural service. According to Clayton C. Hutton he had to be persuaded by the Ministry of Information to abandon his duties in the Fleet Air Arm in order to make *Henry V*.[12] The film came out too late to coincide with D-Day (the date of which had of course been kept secret) but was still dedicated to the troops involved in the Normandy landings.

Those scenes of the film which seem to have made the maximum impact and to have lingered most strongly in the popular imagination (to judge by the number of ill-informed, unresearched published comments I have come across)[13] are those which belong to its patriotic application of the play to the current national crisis: Henry's Churchillian speeches before Harfleur and Agincourt; the dejection, courage and soul-searching of the long night before Agincourt (clearly recalling the mood of 1940); the inserted battle scenes, filmed with all the resources of modern film technology – depicting what Shakespeare's Chorus despaired of depicting: the colourful panoply of chivalry, the glamour of historical pageant, the thrill of victory; the confident, militaristic emotions of 1944. Yet all these details belong to one part of the film: the dramatisation of Acts III and IV of Shakespeare's play; and by themselves do not by any means exhaust or even adequately describe the film's contribution to Shakespeare production.

Shakespeare's Chorus speaks constantly of the difficulties involved in producing an 'epic' drama under Elizabethan stage conditions: the impossibility of presenting with any authenticity or realism the great national events and vivid historical spectacles which constitute the play's ostensible subject:[14]

> But pardon, gentles all,
> The flat unraised spirits that hath dar'd
> On this unworthy scaffold to bring forth
> So great an object: can this cockpit hold
> The vastly fields of France? Or may we cram
> Within this wooden O the very casques
> That did affright the air at Agincourt?

Olivier came to the play equipped with all the formidable technology for portraying reality developed by the modern cinema: all the freedom of the camera to move from interior to exterior, studio to location; all the financial and material resources of setting and costume necessary to provide authentic historical colour; all the technology necessary to film something like the French cavalry charge at Agincourt. Why did Olivier not simply dispense with the Choruses – a testimony to aesthetic limitations long since transcended – and present the film 'realistically' within the conventions of historical reconstruction that Shakespeare's Chorus seems to yearn for? Why, with all these aesthetic resources at command, does the film begin with a reconstruction of an Elizabethan theatre – locking the play back into the constricting framework which its own poetry struggles so hard to escape?

The decision to incorporate into the film devices and aesthetic strategies derived from the dramatic technique of the Chorus provides the film with an ideological tendency which is quite different from – potentially contrary to – its ideology of patriotism, national unity and just war. The film's passage into a 'realistic' reconstruction of Agincourt is mediated by a series of devices which in their different ways distance the art of film from reality, displaying the artificiality of the medium in such a way as to qualify (though not, ultimately, to dispel) the passionate conviction of the patriotic emotion.

The most influential view of the Chorus in *Henry V* is that it is there to give the drama an *epic* character: to enlarge and elevate dramatic spectacle from the conflicts of persons to the conflict of nations, from the limited space of the stage to the territory of international war. The Chorus urges the audience to supply, by a sustained imaginative participation, the kind of scale and realistic narrative detail possible in epic poem and novel, but not in drama. Cued by the Chorus' poetry, the audience can fill in the sense of space and of enormous, farspread human activity (particularly of a military kind) proper to the epic; and thereby provide the necessary context of great achievement, heroic struggle, enormous human effort and significant space, in which the epic hero's destiny can be unfolded and admired. In addition, the Choruses provide the play with a neo-classical unity of action and the didactic purpose of holding up heroic action for admiration and imitation. (Walter, *Henry V*, pp. xiv-xvii).

But the Choruses have a double function. They *are* there to create an epic space for the drama in the imaginations of the audience. But they are there also to draw attention to the *theatrical* nature of this event; a performance, in which history is reshaped and transformed by actors, before an audience, on a stage. The Choruses are there to foreground the *artificiality* of the dramatic event, placing a barrier between action and audience. The audience's imaginations are invited inside that barrier to enjoy direct participation in the drama. At the same time, the play is limiting the freedom of reference from the events on the stage back to ordinary everyday reality.

> A kingdom for a stage, princes to act,
> And monarchs to behold the swelling scene.
> (*Henry V*, Prologue, 3–4)

This does not simply demand an acceptance of certain dramatic conventions, so that kingdoms and princes can easily be substituted in the minds of the audience for the stage and actors. It also declares the artificiality of the dramatic medium, by calling attention to the stage, to the actors and to an audience which knows full well that it is *not* composed entirely of 'monarchs'. The following lines create a vivid imaginative sense (typical of the play's imagery) of a terrifying, barely suppressed brutality; the violence controlled by this militaristic, warlord-king:

> Then should the warlike Henry, like himself,
> Assume the port of Mars; and at his heels,
> Leash'd in like hounds, should famine, sword and fire
> Crouch for employment. (*Henry V*, Prologue, 5-8)

But the roused fear, (drawing, in the images of fire, famine and slaughter, on one of the most brutal passages of Holinshed)[15] is immediately drained off, as the Chorus points to the innocuous mundanity of the stage itself – 'this unworthy scaffold', and of the theatre – 'this wooden O', this 'cockpit'. The phrases contain the violence of the action, and inscribe an imaginary barrier between audience and action.[16] The Chorus to Act IV uses this technique to deflect the violence of Agincourt:

> And so our scene must to the battle fly
> Where, O for pity! we shall much disgrace
> With four or five most vile and ragged foils,
> Right ill-disposed in brawl ridiculous
> The name of Agincourt. Yet sit and see;
> Minding true things by what their mock'ries be.

The way to convince an audience of the truth of dramatic illusion is not, clearly, to insist continually on the illusory nature of the representation. By defining the nature of this dramatic 'mock'ry', the play diminishes rather than enlarges the audience's readiness to receive it as 'true'.

The Choruses are concerned then not so much with bestowing epic qualities on the dramatic event, as with exposing the nature of theatrical illusion. The Chorus has its own kind of heroic language: but it is up to the audience to create an epic experience:

> For 'tis your thoughts that now must deck our kings …

In a play, history is created by a peculiar conjuncture of the dramatist's words, the actor's speech and gesture, and the audience's response. If epic is produced, it is produced only in and by these specific theatrical conditions. There is no heroic view of life to be carried away from the theatre – one that would be confirmed and reflected back by the public morality of society, as for the audiences of Homer or of the Beowulf-poet. *Henry V* insists too strongly, through its Choruses, on the divergence between theatre and real events for any such simple relationship to hold.

Given these factors, it is no surprise to find that in *Henry V* epic qualities and heroic language are bestowed on unpromising material – on events and characters which cannot, in themselves, evoke anything like a wholehearted epic admiration. Patriotism, heroism, chivalry, the romance of war, can induce admiration and delight only when detached from their actual historical context and safely recreated in the security of the theatre purely as ideological entities. Once the real historical foundations of these ideologies are recognised, they lose their power to charm the imagination. The play is concerned both to isolate these ideologies and extract from them the maximum aesthetic and theatrical effect; while at the same time demonstrating the historical actualities from which they are in practice (though not in the theatre) inseparable.

The Chorus' final epilogue both claims and denies the reality, the validity of Henry's achievement: once again foregrounding the theatrical situation, it lavishes praise on Henry in conventional terms:

> Thus far, with rough and all unable pen,
> Our bending author hath pursu'd the story;
> In little room confining mighty men,
> Mangling by starts the full course of their glory.
> Small time, but in that small most greatl'y liv'd
> This star of England: Fortune made his sword,
> By which the world's best garden he achieved,
> And of it left his son imperial lord.
> Harry the Sixth, in infant bands crown'd King
> Of France and England, did this king succeed;
> Whose state so many had the managing,

> That they lost France and made his England bleed:
> Which oft our stage hath shown; and, for their sake,
> In your fair minds let this acceptance take.

Ironically, Shakespeare had written of the events succeeding Henry's reign earlier, in *Henry VI*, 'which oft our stage hath shown': a comparison which neatly distances drama from history. The temporal sequence of events is reversed and the achievements of *Henry V* viewed in the light of the disasters of his son's reign. Henry VI spoke harshly indeed about his father's famous victories:

> But Clifford, tell me, didst thou ever hear
> That things ill got had ever bad success?
> And happy always was it for that son
> Whose father for his hoarding went to hell?
> I'll leave my son my virtuous deeds behind;
> And would my father had left me no more!
>   (*3 Henry VI*, II ii 45–50)

The stage can show Henry's brief triumph as convincingly as it can show his son's tragedy. But while the ironical and pessimistic perspective on history offered by the latter would be confirmed by everyday experience – even the everyday experience of playgoing – the heroic achievement can be created only in the theatre, only by the 'fair minds' of the audience. What has been created here is the reverse of epic, where the hero enacts, for the admiration of the audience, some real problem of public morality; what has been created in this play is a self-mocking dramatic illusion, which inscribes a clear boundary between public morality and the ideological nature of its own 'celebration'.

Various speculations have been attempted about Olivier's motives for locating the drama back into the historical context of the Elizabethan theatre. It has been suggested that the intention was primarily theatrical – to make a film of a stage production, rather than screen adaptation of a play. Or perhaps the motive was more academic – the equivalent of a scholarly appendix on contemporary stage conditions. Or it was an exercise in cultural philanthropy – purveying the cream of high culture to a popular audience? It does not seem to have been realised that the film, in imitating Shakespeare's Chorus, also incorporates some of the aesthetic devices which work within Shakespeare's drama to undermine the play's traditionalist and official ideology.

The film begins with a shot of empty space – a scrap of paper is windblown through a vacant blue sky; whirled towards the camera, it resolves into a handbill advertising a performance of *Henry V* at the Globe Theatre. Insofar as this device demands literal interpretation, it represents exactly that – a handbill tossed by the wind through the sky of Elizabethan London. But that blue sky is also empty space and time: the handbill, before it becomes the title page of a play, is a scrap of paper arbitrarily carried forward from the past, indecipherable until it unfolds before the camera, meaningless until it is *read*. The film seems to begin by suggesting that the play floats in a turbulent vacuum of history until a process of visualisation – of *reproduction* – transforms it into history of a new kind. The faintly disorientating character of this device contrasts sharply with the more familiar evocation of a firm, objectively existent historical tradition which is there to be read off from Shakespeare's text, or the legend of Henry V, or the soul of the English nation.

The camera then displays a reconstructed model (very obviously a model, patently artificial) of Elizabethan London, and a slow crane-shot comes to rest on the Globe Theatre. The camera then penetrates to the interior of the theatre, to show an audience collecting for a performance. A rich assemblage of visual detail seeks to portray a reconstruction of the theatre's atmosphere and tone in a lively, noisy and sociable gathering, with much public self-display of the nobility, the sale of food and drink; all accompanied by William Walton's effective pseudo-Elizabethan music. The performance proper begins, not with a curtain raised to display a naturalistic *mis-en-scène*, but with a boy displaying a large printed card bearing the play's title – a convention of the

Elizabethan theatre (and, incidentally, of Brecht's epic theatre) which disrupts any attempt at naturalistic illusion. There is no attempt at all to translate theatre into film: what is being filmed is a theatre in action. Throughout Shakespeare's Act I the theatrical conditions are visible: sections of the audience, those seated on the stage and those on the floor or in the galleries; the prompter, the tiring room and so on.

Critics committed to the independence of film as an art, and hostile to any dependence of film on the literary media, have shown impatience with what they see as the inappropriate survival here of theatrical form (see Blumenthal, '*Macbeth* into *Throne of Blood*', pp. 191-2; Aicken, 'Shakespeare on the Screen', p. 34).[17] But it is much more important to describe the specific aesthetic and ideological effects of this foregrounding of productive devices. As long as the theatrical context remains visible (up to the end of Shakespeare's Act II) the audience can retain the possibility of seeing Henry primarily as an *actor* rather than as a historical character; and this is much more than the ostentatious virtuosity of a famous screen actor displaying itself before the cameras. With this suggestion supplied, the audience can easily make an imaginative jump from theatre to history: this is a king who seems to rule more by the accomplished deployment of theatrical techniques than by statesmanship or good government. The radical and subversive potentiality of Shakespeare's play consists mainly in this tendency of the drama to call attention to the artificiality of its dramatic devices; and to create a perspective in which the king can display himself as an *actor* rather than a naturalistic character. Our first glimpse of Henry in the film is not on the stage as king, but in the tiring room as a nervous actor, numb with stage-fright, anxiously clearing his throat: prior to making his entrance to immediate and rapturous applause from a noisy and very visible audience. Henry presents himself to the audience as an actor, with scant respect for the conventions of naturalistic drama.

The scene with the clergymen is played as farce, with continual and voluble interventions by the audience: and the high point of Henry's self-dramatisation occurs in the film (as it does in the play) in his reaction to the Dauphin's insulting gift of tennis balls. In this scene the camera employs a device developed by Olivier to overcome some of the difficulties involved in translating drama into film:

> The film climax is a close-up; the Shakespearean climax is a fine gesture and a loud voice. I remember going to George Cukor's *Romeo and Juliet*. As a film director he did what seemed the right thing when he took the potion scene with Norma Shearer – he crept right up to a huge head, the ordinary film climax. But it was in fact a mistake. She, being a good technician in film-making, cut the power of her acting down as the camera approached her for the climax of that speech leading up to taking the potion – 'Romeo. I come! This do I drink to thee'.
>
> At the moment of climax she was acting very smally, because the camera was near. This was not the way it should have been. So the very first test I made for *Henry V* I tried to see how it would work in reverse. It was in the scene with the French Ambassador, and as I raised my voice the camera went back ... (Olivier quoted in Manvell, *Shakespeare and the Film*, pp. 37–8).

Olivier was speaking here primarily of the function of this technique as it concerned the actor: but the device also makes an important contribution to the 'epic' quality of the film, especially in the realistic, exterior location scenes used to represent Agincourt. The movement from close-up to long-shot does not just allow scope for the actor to intensify his performance. It also, more fundamentally, increases the size and multiplies the content of the frame, and supplies more abundance of visual detail thereby bringing more objects, images and characters into significant relationship. Henry's 'Crispian Crispian' speech (IV.iii) before Agincourt begins as a close shot from below depicting Henry himself (whose face, in close-up and soliloquy, has been dominating the screen in the previous sequence): as his speech rises to a climax the camera pulls back and up, to reveal the assembled masses of fighting men around him, all excited by his militaristic rhetoric and infected with his martial enthusiasm. The frame expands from a focus on the leader's personality, to an image of the leader as centre of his loyal army: from the psychological to the epic, from the monarch to the nation.

The same technique, used to film the earlier scene with the French Ambassador, has an entirely different effect. A close-up shot shows Henry's controlled passion of indignation at the Dauphin's insult. As his speech of reply (I. ii. 259-97) rises to a climax, the camera pulls back to reveal, not a naturalistic social setting, but a stage, other costumed actors, an audience, a theatre. The effect is heightened by a deliberate emphasis on Henry as an actor playing to the audience: one shot taken from the back of the stage displays him *acting* before his enthusiastic spectators. His exit line at the end of the scene is delivered as a flourish directly to the audience.

As in Shakespeare's play, then, complete with its alienating device of the Chorus, the king can be characterised as an *actor* rather than a monarch: the drama displays his capacity to masquerade and perform, his ability to generate acclamation and excitement in the *theatrical* context. The *playing* is very obviously *play*. To see this, as many have done, as a naturalistic method of presenting theatre on the screen, is to seriously underestimate the subtlety of the film's aesthetic devices; to see the film as concerned simply to offer a 'straight' patriotic version of *Henry V* is to interpret selected parts rather than the film's significant whole.

Consider, for example, the effect of interpolating the scene of Falstaff's death. This is played, and filmed, very 'straight': it is the point where the visible theatrical framework gives way to the painted backdrop scenery and realistic locations of the later sequences; and it is deprived of all Shakespeare's humour. The effect aimed at by invented action, text, visual image and music, is one of overwhelming pathos. Falstaff is shown on his death-bed: he rouses faintly to repeat his lines from *Henry IV Part Two*:

> God save thy Grace, King Hal, my royal Hal!
> … God save thee, my sweet boy!   (*Henry IV*, 2. V. v. 41–3)

The grim tones of the new king's reply appear in voice-over: 'I know thee not, old man'. Falstaff falls back, flocculates and expires. The scene closes with a shot from outside the chamber window: a curtain is drawn across it. Meanwhile, we hear Pistol and his companions departing for the war; Pistol quotes, in another interesting interpolation, lines from Marlowe's *Tamburlaine*:

> Is it not passing brave to be a king
> And ride in triumph through Persepolis?

The theatrical metaphors are very obvious here, and very much in the spirit of Shakespeare's play. The drawn curtain marks the end, not so much of Falstaff's life, as of his role. Has the king destroyed him because he cannot tolerate such theatrical competition; because he will not be upstaged by his former comrade? Pistol's main function in Shakespeare's play is to parody, by projecting a Marlovian megalomania, the king's tendency to dramatise himself as the old-fashioned epic hero. His interpolated *Tamburlaine* echo is taken up and confirmed by the next film scene, which contains a brief precis of II ii at Southampton, with the Earl of Cambridge's conspiracy completely removed. Henry is shown dramatising himself as crusader, military leader, would-be conquering hero – and very much enjoying his role. The immediate juxtaposition of this colourful pageant with the melancholy chiaroscuro of Falstaff's death supplies an undertone of calculated cruelty to Henry's extravagant display of theatrical virtuosity. Evidently it *is* passing brave to be a king, and ride in triumph through Persepolis; though it is passing unfair to be a rejected and betrayed companion, and die in loneliness and poverty.

Once the film settles into realistic locations for the battle of Agincourt (locations which occupy a small part of the film, yet which have, significantly, attracted a disproportionate amount of attention) the theatrical framework disappears completely, and with it the film's radical and subversive potentialities. The viewer is immersed in a *real* world which becomes increasingly analogous to the world of contemporary history. Scenes such as that between Henry and the soldiers (IVi) with all the fear and anxiety of a night before battle – the naturalistically presented military action showing the defensive preparation of the English and the showy chivalry of the French – were evidently too close to the contemporary experience of war for the film to free itself from, or even to offer qualification of, what becomes its dominant ideology. *Action* replaces *acting*; the serious business of fighting suppresses the freedom of theatrical play; the world of the film becomes more like the Britain of 1940. The critical exigencies of the contemporary situation pull the film back, away from its aesthetic experiments, into complicity with the ideologies of patriotism, war enthusiasm and national unity. This suspension of the viewer's complex awareness of the theatrical event, this immersion of the viewer into a carefully constructed facsimile of a 'real' world, is so successful that it is with a shock that we see the theatre reappear at the end. The illusions of naturalism and of conventional theatre have temporarily succeeded in dominating the spectator's imagination: and through the selectivity of collective memory have enabled the film to be incorporated more readily into the prevailing mythology of Britain at war.

る

All criticism of the histories emanates from E.M.W. Tillyard's pioneering work, *Shakespeare's History Plays* (1944). Whether one agrees or disagrees with it, Tillyard's has become the traditional interpretation of the history plays.[18]

Tillyard's study, despite sharing a common subject, common preoccupations and – ultimately – a common ideology, differs signally from the other two texts in displaying an apparent innocence of contemporary engagement. The study is purely a discourse of academic scholarship, giving the impression that a characteristic and central activity of English culture has been quietly proceeding, unravaged by the fierce reality of world history. While Knight and Olivier were reconstructing Shakespeare to point his relevance to the nation's crisis, Tillyard, with a gesture of academic indifference to contemporary events, was patiently clearing the earth of history from the roots of English culture, re-establishing a continuity with the Elizabethan age unbroken by crisis, war, threatened invasion; though his affirmation of continuity is nowhere explicitly admitted.

Tillyard's major argument – the legacy of which determined almost all subsequent criticism of the history plays, and dominated school examining for decades – is that of *order*. The ideological sources of Shakespeare's history plays lay in dominant traditions of contemporary thought, expressed in historiographical and philosophical writings of the Tudor and Elizabethan period. These asserted that the existing political state, the 'body politic', could not be considered merely as a particular form of social organisation, but was in reality a function of a universal order, created and supervised by God; ruled over, ultimately, by divine providence. A state or human society occupied a median position in a cosmic hierarchy, with God and the angels above, and the animal and plant kingdoms below. The structure of a well-ordered state was itself a microcosm of the hierarchical cosmos – containing within itself a chain of being, from the monarch at the head, through various gradations of social rank down to the lowest orders. The ruler of a body politic possessed power which reflected, but was also subject to, that of God: a king therefore ruled implicitly by divine right. The natural condition of a state, like the natural condition of the cosmos, was order, defined primarily in terms of the maintenance of this rigid hierarchy. Any rupturing of this pattern would produce chaos – since the state was a component of a divine order, such alteration could not be mere social change, but a disruption of a divine and natural order, to the displeasure of God and the destruction of universal law. The extreme forms of such disruption, such as the deposition of a king and the usurpation of a throne, would constitute a gross violation of order, inevitably to be punished by the vengeance of God, operating through the workings of divine providence.

According to Tillyard, this doctrine of order was a dominant Elizabethan ideology. Even the teaching of so influential a thinker as Machiavelli with his view that 'disorder' was the natural state of man', meant little to Shakespeare's contemporaries.

> Such a way of thinking was abhorrent to the Elizabethans, (as indeed it always has been and is now to the majority) who preferred to think of order as the norm to which disorder, though lamentably common, was yet the exception.
>
> (Tillyard, p. 21)

This ideology (which, we notice, is *still*, in Tillyard's view, a 'majority' opinion) was Shakespeare's.

> In his most violent representations of chaos Shakespeare never tries to persuade that it is the norm: however long and violent is its sway, it is unnatural; and in the end order and the natural law will reassert themselves.
>
> ... it is not likely that anyone will question my conclusion that Shakespeare's Histories, with their constant pictures of disorder cannot be understood without assuming a larger principle of order in the background ... In the total sequence of his plays dealing with the subject-matter of Hall he expressed successfully a universally held and still comprehensible scheme of history: a scheme fundamentally religious, by which events evolve under a law of justice and under the ruling of God's providence, and of which Elizabethan England was the acknowledged outcome
>
> (Tillyard, *Shakespeare's History Plays*, p. 23, pp. 320–1)

Tillyard asserts what appear to be historical facts about a long-vanished age: there is little to suggest that his concern with 'order' – an unspecified and politically ambiguous vision of society – belongs as much to war-time Britain as to Elizabethan England. He never betrays any suggestion that his universal political moral might have relevance to his own time: though it clearly belongs with Wilson Knight's celebration of 'national unity'. The nearest Tillyard comes to an acknowledgement of the claims of contemporary history is this kind of ambiguous aside – discussing the tradition of sentimentalising Falstaff, he attributes it to Victorian military optimism:

> The sense of security created in nineteenth century England by the predominance of the British navy induced men to rate that very security too cheaply and to exalt the instinct of rebellion above its legitimate station. They forget the threat of disorder which was ever present with the Elizabethans. Schooled by recent events, we should have no difficulty now in talking Falstaff as the Elizabethans took him (Tillyard, *Shakespeare's History Plays*, p. 291)

The word 'schooled' matches the ambiguous portentousness of the academic mannerism: participation in history is a matter of education in moral and political wisdom. What Tillyard means by 'recent events' is unclear. 'Rebellion' could refer to the ascension and territorial expansion of fascism. Or it may more probably refer, as Wilson Knight refers, to the paramount necessity for maintaining order and national unity in face of the threat of foreign conquest. 'We' in 1944, in other words, have as much reason to value order, national unity, a strong but humane monarchy, as did the Elizabethans and Shakespeare.

Such an aside is, however, a flaw in the seamless unity of Tillyard's ideology, which masks its essential conservatism in an impenetrable disguise of academic scholarship. The object we are required to contemplate is not Tillyard thinking about *his* England (as Wilson Knight and Olivier openly declared their patriotic loyalties) but Shakespeare thinking about his:

> *Henry IV* shows a stable society and it is crowded, like no other play of Shakespeare, with pictures of life as it was lived in the age of Elizabeth ... Those who, like myself, believe that Shakespeare had a massively reflective as well as a brilliantly opportunistic

brain will expect these matters of Elizabethan life to serve more than one end and will not be surprised if through them he expresses his own feelings about his fatherland. It is also perfectly natural that Shakespeare should have chosen this particular point in the total stretch of history he covered, as suited to this expression. Henry V was traditionally not only the perfect king, but a king after the Englishmen's heart; one who added the quality of good mixer to the specifically regal virtues. The picture of England would be connected with the typical English monarch (Tillyard, *Shakespeare's History Plays*, p. 299)

The concept of Renaissance England as a well-ordered state is, however, infused with a sentimental attachment to the 'everyday' life of England dramatised in *Henry IV Part Two*: into Tillyard's discourse penetrates an emotional tone which declares, unmistakably, that Shakespeare's 'fatherland' is also his. This 'epic' drama offers a comprehensive cross-section of English life, linking the monarchy with the essential, unchanging rhythm of traditional rural society. The emphasis on the enduring quality of traditional social patterns is confirmed by Tillyard's quoting of Hardy's *In Time of the Breaking of Nations*:

> This will go onward the same
> Though Dynasties pass.
>
> … From first to last Shakespeare was loyal to the country life. He took it for granted as the norm, as the background before which the more formal or spectacular events were transacted (Tillyard, *Shakespeare's History Plays*, p. 302)

or in the words of the popular song: 'There'll always be an England … '. The argument and the quotation deliver us back into that organic, immutable 'English' society: a golden age which, though vanished, can yet linger and survive, unravaged by the fierce historical crisis of the present.

The remarkable logical slide from a description of Renaissance ideology to the celebration of an apparently immutable social and cultural entity called 'England', is Tillyard's most effective ideological strategy: it is, in fact, the quality which ensured that of all the cultural interventions of this period, Tillyard's piece of formal *criticism* would survive as the seminal, determinant text. Without making any explicit acknowledgement of the fact that the England of the Second World War is as much an object of address as that of the sixteenth century, Tillyard invokes and affirms values which were being assiduously – and much more openly – cultivated, especially by the works already discussed.

The general Elizabethan philosophy of 'order' is regarded as the basic structure of all fifteenth/sixteenth century historiographical writing; the metaphysical dialectic of 'order' and 'disorder' was observed in the process of English history, and explained in terms of the ruling idea of providence. The deposition and murder of Richard II was seen as a violation of natural order: the perpetrators of it earned the punishment of divine vengeance, which was also visited generally on the nation as a whole. This pattern Tillyard detected in the chronicles of Holinshed and Hall, the historical narratives of Daniel and *The Mirror for Magistrates*, in the whole *genre* of the Elizabethan history play, and in Shakespeare.

The ideological structure which emerges from this application is what Tillyard (and after him generations of 'A'level candidates) agree to call 'the theme of England': a preoccupation derived from the Morality play, in which 'Respublica', the state, can occupy a central position as character or even hero. Shakespeare's 'theme of England' is in one sense historical – a vision of the providential pattern implicit in the development of a historical process from Richard II to Henry VII – but in a larger sense it is what Tillyard calls 'epic' – a dramatisation of the whole texture and experience of English life, lived between the reality of 'disorder' (dynastic struggle, rebellion, civil war) and the potentiality of 'order' (a static and hierarchical but well-governed state). Just as the great 'order' of the cosmos supervises and contains its internal 'disorder'; so the upheavals of English society between 1399 and 1485 are constrained within a grand conception of the 'order' which the nation really represents:

The theme of Respublica, now given a new turn and treating not merely the future but the very nature of England, what I am calling the epic theme, is subtly contrived ... the theme of England grows naturally till its full compass is reached when Henry V, the perfect English king, comes to the throne. If we were in doubt about the Prince's decision, we should not have the mental repose necessary for appreciating a static picture of England: we should be obsessed, as we are in *Henry VI*, with the events of civil war; and the troubles of Henry IV would quench our interest in the drone of the Lincolnshire bagpipe or the price of stock at Stamford fair

... inspired ... by his own genius, he combined with the grim didactic exposition of the fortunes of England during her terrible ordeal of civil war his epic version of what England was ...
(Tillyard, *Shakespeare's History Plays*, pp. 298–9, p. 263)

The indispensable key to political 'order' is the sovereign – as God's deputy the king must accept high responsibilities, and the man must be fitted to the office. Tillyard regards the two parts of *Henry IV* as in one sense an account of Prince Hal's training for office. The Prince is Shakespeare's ideal portrayal of the 'kingly type': a well-governed personality who confronts 'disorder' (in the form of Falstaff) only to understand and reject it; and who thereby equips himself to govern and embody the 'order' of the state:

The Prince is depicted in *Henry IV* ... as a man of large powers, Olympian loftiness, and high sophistication, who has acquired a thorough knowledge of human nature both in himself and in others. He is Shakespeare's studied picture of the kingly type ...
(Tillyard, *Shakespeare's History Plays*, p. 269)

Tillyard has nothing to reproach the Prince with: his behaviour is always exemplary, a model of what history requires of him. One illustration of this scheme of princely education is the scene in which Hal mocks and manipulates Francis the drawer:

Why should the Prince, after Francis has given him his heart ... join with Poins to put him through a brutal piece of horseplay? ...

The answer is first that the Prince wanted to see just how little
brain Francis had and puts him to the test, and secondly that in
matters of humanity we must not judge Shakespeare by standards
of twentieth century humanitarianism ... Further we must
remember the principle of degree ... The subhuman element in
the population must have been considerable in Shakespeare's day:
that it should be treated almost like beasts was taken for granted
(Tillyard, *Shakespeare's History Plays*, pp. 276-7)

Tillyard draws a clear distinction here between Renaissance attitudes and the standards of 'twentieth century humanitarianism':
a qualification which would, if consistently applied, break the
tacit link between his celebration of Elizabethan 'order' and the
implicit conservatism of the book's ideology. Tillyard, however,
dissociates himself from that 'humanitarianism', not only in his
attempt at an imaginative penetration into the psychology of a
historically remote civilisation, but in his casual use of a phrase
like 'subhuman' – which seems to belong more to the fastidious
class-bound vision of a Cambridge critic, than to the author of
King Lear.

Tillyard does not think highly of *Henry V*. He believes the
character to be quite inconsistent with the Prince Hal of *Henry
IV*, and the play itself to be forced and mechanical. A shying-away
from the robust patriotism embraced by Wilson Knight and
Olivier is characteristic of Tillyard: writing at a time when the
epic heroism of the past could easily be affirmed as living in the
present, the scholar relegates it to an inferior status: the play
about the nature of 'England' is more important than a play
about the military victories of a warrior-king. Tillyard's business
was not with winning the war but with reconstituting the national culture in expectation of an Allied victory.

The influence of Tillyard's study in constituting Shakespeare's
history plays is undeniable – his unitary view of 'order' as the
frame within which 'disorder' is contained was developed with
greater subtlety by D.A. Traversi in *Shakespeare from Richard II
to Henry V*,[19] into a dialectic of order and disorder. Traversi's

endless paradoxes present the plays as agents of reconciliation, balancing and synthesising contradictory views. Even a much later critical work, which advertised itself as having broken the Tillyard mould entirely, betrayed its true ancestry: John Wilders' *The Lost Garden*[20] was a mirror-image of Tillyard's vision, in which 'order' appears as a temporary statis in a process of universal, eternal 'disorder'.

A survey of the historical moment of Tillyard's production reveals that it stood in competition with other forms of cultural intervention in some ways more promising and powerful as strategies of ideological constitution. The timeless work of scholarship shares a common ideology with other works which confronted their society much more openly, addressed its problems much more directly, made no secret of the ideological foundation of their cultural productions. Wilson Knight made serious efforts to insert Shakespeare's prophetic vision directly into the texture of national life. He gave readings from Shakespeare with his own commentaries; and in July 1941, at the Westminster Theatre, staged a bizarre production called *This Sceptred Isle*, which involved the actor Henry Ainley reading Knight's commentaries (from off-stage) and Knight himself acting various speeches from Shakespeare, under headings like 'St. George for England' and 'The Royal Phoenix'. The programme announced the production as 'G. Wilson Knight's dramatisation of Shakespeare's Call to Great Britain in Time of War'. Olivier's role in *Henry V* was indistinguishable (apart from the uniform) from his real-life role as patriotic orator, a Churchillian inspiration to the Home Front. In each case there is a serious attempt to address the question of national unity directly, and to convey it through the more immediate, accessible and popular media of theatre, public reading and film.

Wilson Knight's grotesque patriotism and Olivier's martial rhetoric are now consigned to the margins of literary history: yet Tillyard's equally strange discovery of a governing philosophy of 'order' in Elizabethan society and in Shakespeare's plays, lives on as a potent ideological force. Evidently, the more *ideological* a work of criticism is (in the sense of its involving strong elements of concealment, deception and mystification) the more effective it will be in the long run as a constitutive element of cultural history. To declare a position too openly, as Wilson Knight did, is to render the work vulnerable as criticism: to talk of Shakespeare writing a 'call to arms' for Britain in 1944, or predicting expansion of British power into world-order through ventures like the Falklands campaign, is to acknowledge far too openly that 'literature' is here being *invented* by the critic to serve a specific, contemporary, political purpose. The case of the Olivier film is different: though it also shows its hand by explicitly drawing analogies with the Second World War, it also contains elements which render it vulnerable in other ways. While its virile patriotism needs to be pushed into one margin of cultural history, it contains elements which demand marginalisation in the opposite direction: its experimental foregrounding of aesthetic devices constitutes a subversive tendency which might well call into question the simplicity of its patriotic affirmations.

The distinctive quality of Tillyard's work is evidently its denial of contemporary history, its apparently timeless innocence of political orientation. Where Wilson Knight and Olivier declared, in their different ways, that Britain in her hour of need could turn to Shakespeare, Tillyard quietly affirmed that Shakespeare has always been, is, and always will be 'England'. The effectiveness of the enterprise can be measured by the fact that assent to that proposition can seem like recognition of the long familiar. Shakespeare has 'always' been the national poet, identifiable with the greatest age of our history: what could seem more 'natural' than to invoke his presence in a time of national peril? Such familiarising, with its absence of any explicit avowal of a determinant historical context, was peculiarly well adapted to the task of establishing an image of 'Shakespeare's England' which would serve as an ideological power of social cohesion in Churchill's Britain. The scholarly imagination, revisiting a vanished past, severs the history it addresses from the exigencies of the present; and thus insidiously operates on the reader who, aware only of the attention he or she focuses on Shakespeare, is quite unaware of how an image of his or her own society is being implicitly celebrated and affirmed.

Many people felt during the Second World War that they were fighting for a new society of democracy, peace and justice: that the ordeal of the war could be made tolerable by assurance that the old society of poverty, inequality, unemployment, could never return. Tillyard offered his readers a different reason for fighting and enduring: to defend the society which existed once, still remains (implicitly) the 'natural' form of political order, and is visible in the works of Shakespeare. In the Labour victory of 1945, it seemed that the old world lay in ruins and was decisively rejected by the people. E.M.W. Tillyard's *Shakespeare's History Plays* was reprinted in 1948, 1951, 1956, 1959, 1961, 1964, 1969 and 1974.

CHAPTER SIX

The Taming of the Shrew (1989)

જ્જ

T HEATRE AND FILM are both media of 'performance', yet
the technological and theoretical differences between them
are radical and profound. The preceding pages have frequently
deployed the familiar distinction between a play as literary textualisation and as living enactment: on the one hand the printed
text, apparently permanently fixed and immobile, resistant to
intervention or participation, inviting the kind of reading that
seeks the intended coherence of authorial meaning; on the other,
the ephemeral medium of theatrical performance, an experiential
form concerned with the shaping of a malleable material, open to
contribution from performers and audience alike, a collaborative enterprise of production and interpretation. Film and theatre
can be thought of as so naturally complementary that the translation of a play from one to another – the feature film developed
from a stage production or the videotape of a live performance
– is a smooth and unproblematic process.

In fact, the medium of film, at least in terms of the social and
cultural uses to which the technology has traditionally been put,
has more in common in this context with literature than with
drama. Clearly the processes of theatrical and film adaptation
have equal liberty to interpret and reconstruct a dramatic
text; both theoretically 'free', both subject to the pressures and

determinants of any socio-cultural situation. The process by which a 'text' is turned into a 'performance' through analysis, discussion, interpretative experiment, improvisation and rehearsal, may be very similar in each case. Yet although in a film a play is being enacted by living performers, that concrete human realisation is overridden by the finality of the finished product: the enactment is then fixed and frozen in a perpetually mobile immobility. In a theatrical space actors may be empowered to continue interpreting the dramatic text in an experimental process of discovery and improvisation; in a film, whatever procedures of rehearsal and exploration may precede the final shooting, the entire product of the actors' communication is arrested at the point of editing. In a theatre an audience is present at the dramatic event, participating in the performance in whatever manner may be permitted by the nature of the theatrical space and the relations between actors and audience; in a cinema the spectator is present at the image of an absent event, illuminatingly shadowed by the two-dimensional phantasmagoria of the screen.

Of course this distinction deals with potentialities rather than with innate and inevitable characteristics of the respective media. A convention-bound theatrical performance, or one which is choreographed to the point of fossilisation, can approach as closely to the resistant fixity of literature as a naturalistic film; and a more experimental filmic medium can realise in concrete form some of the pluralistic potentialities still present in the discourse of 'script' or 'screenplay'. Having proposed a global theoretical distinction between the two performance media, we can move to a further distinction between conservative and experimental discourses within each medium: and within that distinction it is possible to discover a parallel, between the pictorial realism of nineteenth-century staging, and the naturalistic tendency of certain kinds of film.

If the introduction of perspective scenery and pictorial sets was a means of bringing the theatre closer to the representation of reality, then clearly the medium of film immediately outstripped the imitative technology of the stage. Film was able not only to portray reality more convincingly through the use of studio sets: it could also represent physical reality itself directly through location shooting. Early silent films of Shakespeare plays have been treated by film historians and critics with enormous condescension, as little more than a crude rehearsal for the artistic and technological flowering of the talkies. This misjudgement is a typical undervaluing of the visual elements of drama, and a misunderstanding of the historical development of silent film. For most of the nineteenth century only the privileged patent theatres were permitted to use the verbal texts of serious drama, with the result that elsewhere the theatre had been obliged to develop a primarily visual and musical discourse (*melo-drama*) with which to communicate the plays. Silent film simply appropriated this theatrical language and realised it through a pictorial naturalism of visual style and the deployment of mime techniques in acting.

This historical link between the nineteenth-century pictorial stage and the medium of film has also received theoretical attention. Catherine Belsey has argued that film is 'the final realisation of the project of perspective staging', and that both stand in fundamental confrontation with the theatrical language of the Renaissance public playhouse.[1] I have argued in Chapter Three that this fixing of interpretation and privileging of the single point of view is not a *necessary* effect of film, which as a medium has the technological resources to resist such 'textualisation'. It is nonetheless clear that a film which invites or endorses complicity with the techniques of the proscenium arch and pictorial stage runs the risk of surrendering from the play those pluralistic capacities guaranteed it by the architectural space of its original performance. It is likely to localise what should be unlocalised; concretise what should be left open to the imagination; represent what should be distanced, and naturalise what should be estranged. Franco Zeffirelli's film version of *The Taming of the Shrew*, best known as a naturalistic and pictorial treatment of the play, requires serious consideration in the terms of this theoretical problem.

The critical discourses available for description, analysis and interpretation of a stage version of a Shakespeare play derive from literary criticism, theatrical reviewing, and specifically dramatic perspectives such as those of theatre history and the semiotics of drama. A genuinely *filmed* version of a Shakespeare play (as distinct from a filmed stage version) invites interpretative response from film criticism and theory as well as from the literary and dramatic approaches. This conjuncture creates particular difficulties, since the mainstream of film criticism, unlike the methodologies of other disciplines, is highly theoretical, avant-garde and internationalist, where literary and dramatic criticism tend predominantly to be empirical, conservative and chauvinistic. Film criticism has thoroughly absorbed the influences of the post-structuralist revolution in cultural theory, and concerns itself with genre studies, popular culture, semiotics; with experimental rather than traditional work; and with cinema as a global language with a world-wide constituency. To many exponents of film criticism a film of a Shakespeare play is not truly a film at all, but a hybrid amalgamation of two hostile cultural discourses, tainted by the noxious traces of the stage, of high art, of cultural élitism and of British cultural imperialism. Critical work on Shakespeare films has been produced on that marginal terrain of literary and dramatic studies where film and television are employed in an essentially ancillary manner to support a critical enterprise centred on text and theatrical realisation.

From that marginal space emerge voices articulating cultural contradiction and divided loyalty. It has become a commonplace in the criticism of Shakespeare films that the Renaissance play and the filmic medium are radically dissimilar and in some fundamental ways incompatible. Yet almost all such criticism insists on interpreting and evaluating a Shakespeare film in comparison with the 'original' textual inscription. Starting from the premise that a piece of sixteenth-century dramatic literature fiercely resists translation into a twentieth-century technological medium, critics nonetheless reserve the right to castigate a film for failing to realise 'Shakespeare'. Here, for example, is a formulation of the key distinction between stage and film to which all writers on film would have to assent:

> If Racine, Shakespeare or Molière cannot be brought to the cinema by just placing them before the camera and the microphone, it is because the handling of the action and the style of the dialogue were conceived as echoing through the architecture of the auditorium. What is specifically theatrical about these tragedies is not their action so much as the human, that is to say the verbal, priority given to their dramatic structure. The problem of filmed theatre at least where the classics are concerned does not consist so much in transposing an action from the stage to the screen as in transposing a text written for one dramaturgical system into another while at the same time retaining its effectiveness.[2]

Yet here is a characteristically hostile critique of Zeffirelli's *Taming of the Shrew* which first concedes, and then simply ignores, this distinction:

> True, this is a film, not a play, and must be judged on its own terms, but no one with an understanding of the relation of the parts to the whole in a successful work could effectively hope to make a good film using the playwright's words in so significantly altered a setting.
>
> Zeffirelli's next project is *Romeo and Juliet* as a *ciné-verité* documentary on Renaissance Verona. Which takes us back to the very first point: one can't help feeling that only a man without a concept of the way parts of an art work relate to the whole could cherish this ambition; or a man who neither understands nor profoundly likes Shakespeare for what he is.[3]

My discussion of this particular example of filmed Shakespeare will thus be dogged by this theoretical impasse between stage and screen. I will attempt to evaluate Zeffirelli's production in its own specifically *filmic* terms rather than in comparison with some ideal mode of an authoritatively Shakespearean realisation.

To think of Zeffirelli purely as a film director is an oversimplification. He began his career studying architecture and stage design in Florence; became first an actor and then a costume- and set-designer in the theatre; worked as a film technician with masters of the Italian cinema such as Luchino Visconti; designed and directed operas; and came to the filming of Shakespeare through successful attempts to direct the plays in the theatre – his other Shakespeare film *Romeo and Juliet* (1968) began its long gestation as a stage production at the Old Vic in 1960. Recently he has filmed opera with *La Traviata* and on stage designed, directed and filmed Verdi's *Otello*. It would be difficult to imagine a career better calculated to place a director in the ideal position to make a film of a Shakespeare play. But Zeffirelli's conception of Shakespeare is very unlike that restless curiosity about the intrinsic potentialities of the text and its filmic capacities that we associate with Laurence Olivier. He appears more inclined towards a European's formal respect for the virtues of classical 'English' theatre. That notion of the classic, its artistic value and moral potency, forms an element in a humanistic aesthetic concerned with the potential unity of European culture. When invited by the Old Vic to direct in England, Zeffirelli confessed to an idealistic view of the project as a synthesis of modern Italian emotions with classical English values:

> I had worked in England presenting Italian works and the real satisfaction I took back to Italy was simply that I had helped a little towards a better understanding of its culture by the English.
>
> Now I have an even more interesting task – a combination of Italian feelings applied to a masterpiece of the classical English theatre which might prove, if successful, that times have changed in Europe and people of different backgrounds can easily work together for creating a new European conscience.
>
> This is to me far more important than any diplomatic or political manoeuvres.[4]

This liberal-humanist internationalism links the cultural theory of an earlier age with the political alliances of a later: an aesthetic superstructure for the Treaty of Rome. Zeffirelli's much-quoted sentiments indicate a number of priorities and preoccupations governing his approach to Shakespeare: a formal reverence for the masterpieces of the classical past, which can paradoxically, in its celebration of cultural continuity, involve a lack of interest in the formal properties of those masterpieces; a view of theatrical work as a kind of cultural diplomacy, fostering international understanding and sympathy through the European community; a real concern with a broad popular audience; and a subordination of historical interest in the Elizabethan drama to a vision of its mobilisation in the service of contemporary socio-cultural unity. Where Zeffirelli is deeply interested in history – and this has important implications for his production of the *Shrew* – it is the history of his own Italian culture rather than that of the English Renaissance: to him Shakespeare serves as a bridge between a classical past and the immediate preoccupations of the present.

It is not only as a film maker therefore that Zeffirelli regarded Shakespeare as fair game for a contemporary appropriation. His naturalistic aesthetic (owing more to the 'neo-realist' *ciné-verité* of Italian movies than to the traditional fictional or theatrical realisms of Zola and Giovanni Verga) is directed firmly towards a rendering of the classical heritage into forms immediate and comprehensible to modern experience. This aspiration involved a particular emphasis on the young, both as participants and spectators; since it was contemporary youth that Zeffirelli hoped to engage as an audience for both his theatrical and film productions. His film of *Romeo and Juliet* stands as the most obvious example of an attempt to communicate directly with young people through a drama of adolescent passion: casting the teenagers Leonard Whiting and Olivia Hussey as the lovers, Zeffirelli subordinated his respect for the classical virtues to a naturalistic emphasis on identification and vicarious experience. When John Francis Lane visited the set of *The Taming of the Shrew* in Rome during the making of the film, he found himself 'intruding on an undergraduate "rag", the type of student jam-boree which has been a feature of university life in all Europe's seats of learning from the Middle Ages to the 1960s'.[5] Though the *Shrew* is based on a stock 'New Comedy' situation involving con-flict between generations, it is hardly a drama of teenage passion and misunderstanding: so the mobilisation of adolescent masses for this play was evidently symptomatic of Zeffirelli's insistence on communicating the play to a youthful audience. The under-graduate 'rag' became the film's opening sequence; in order to compose it Zeffirelli recruited the fashionably disaffected adoles-cents of Rome for a crowd scene. He advertised in local papers inviting the local *capelloni* (literally 'long-haired ones') to come for auditions, and transformed them into the undergraduates of Renaissance Padua.

> Zeffirelli conceived the film as a bridge between Renaissance Italy and Elizabethan England; but also between the lusty ribald way of life of those times and the no less vigorous 'swinging' world of our own day. The kids who let off steam in fifteenth-century Padua are shown to be just as full of sprits as the lads and lasses of Pope Paul's Rome or Harold Wilson's London. It is not surprising to learn that Zeffirelli's favourite film of last year was not one of the sacred masterpieces of Jean-Luc Godard. It was *Help!* (Lane, *Films and Filming*, pp. 51-2)

The Italianising of Shakespeare which earned the director the ironical title of 'Shakespirelli' ('What Zeffirelli is aiming at is to restore the Italian Renaissance spirit to Shakespeare', Lane, p.52) goes hand in hand with a determined spirit of modernisation: Zeffirelli's 'Pop-Shakespeare' productions were designed to speak to a younger generation as eloquently as the Beatles' film *Help!* According to John Francis Lane, this ambition was clearly being realised: 'Above all, the young Italians are packing the playhouses to see his Shakespeare productions. Some youngsters who had never seen Shakespeare before … are startled to find that Shakespirelli's Romeo and Juliet behave like two young people of today' (Lane, *Films and Filming*, p. 52).

These are some of the reasons why Zeffirelli's film versions of Shakespeare are probably among the most enduringly popular of such productions. The other obvious reasons have little to do with youth, and more with Zeffirelli's success in organising the 'production' side of the film, integrating it firmly into the power-structure of the cinema industry. The economic buoyancy of the entire project compares interestingly with Orson Welles' protract-ed and impoverished struggles to make, for example, *Othello*: and this favourable commercial climate for the *Shrew* evidently owed much to the wealthy and successful 'stars' of the film, Richard Burton and Elizabeth Taylor, who also acted as co-producers, investing over 3 million dollars. Richard Roud of the *Guardian* reflected ironically on the cultural-commercial alliances that formed the infrastructure of this particular realisation of Shakespeare on film:

> When the Carnegies and the Rockefellers had all made their pack-ets, their thoughts began to turn to culture. They built libraries, founded foundations, and created cultural centres. This is a recog-nised pattern in America, and one that is even encouraged by the tax laws. So it would be churlish to reproach the Burtons – Richard and Elizabeth – for simply having followed the custom of their adopted country. After the *Butterfield 8*s, the *Cleopatras*, they now can offer us *Dr Faustus*, possibly even a *Romeo and Juliet*. This week we are faced with the first of their cultural enterprises for the cinema: *The Taming of the Shrew*.[6]

Both *The Taming of the Shrew* and *Romeo and Juliet* were pre-miered, in 1966 and 1968, as Royal Command Performances before, respectively, Princess Margaret and Her Majesty the Queen.

❧

It could occasion little surprise, in view of Zeffirelli's credentials as a naturalistic director, that he would find no use for Shakespeare's 'Induction' or the Christopher Sly framework. As Jack Jorgens observes, 'Whatever ironic perspective Shakespeare provided by making the main action a crude entertainment for a drunken, deluded tinker trying in vain to get his "wife" into bed is gone, for like many theatrical directors, Zeffirelli has omitted the frame-story altogether'.[7] In its place Zeffirelli supplied his own 'induction', in the form of the fifteenth-century 'student rag' described above. Jack Jorgens describes the opening sequence:

> *Padua.* Lucentio and Tranio ride through lush countryside, arriving in a busy Renaissance city. Occupied with a huge blonde whore, Tranio loses his master in the crowd. Titles over university choir singing sombre music, students being blessed in a cathedral. Festive music as students run wild in streets in masks, waving banners, conducting mock funeral, mimicking blonde Bianca as she is bawdily serenaded by gallants: 'Give me leave/To do for thee all that Adam did for Eve.' Bianca, summoned home, is chased by Lucentio and Tranio, Gremio and Hortensio. (Jorgens, *Shakespeare and Film*, p. 259)

Thus the film modulates into the first of its many farcical chases – it ends with Petruchio still chasing an irrepressibly escaping Kate – via the dramatisation of a ritual of celebration considerably older than (though conjecturally the ancestor of) the 1960s undergraduate 'rag'. The collapse of an ecclesiastical service into merciless parody (the 'mock funeral'), unrestrained revelry and orgiastic release is Zeffirelli's attempt to reconstruct the carnivals of the Middle Ages. Our contemporary rediscovery of the cultural theory of Mikhail Bakhtin[8] has made 'carnival' a key concept in the analysis of all medieval and Renaissance dramatic art: Zeffirelli simply tapped the resources of his own national history to produce a detailed evocation of saturnalian ritual[9]. In the course of the opening sequence (framed as an 'induction' by the superimposition of film titles), we observe the barbaric anti-ceremony of clerics wearing grotesque animal masks, sacred music giving way to obscene and cacophonous chants, a blasphemously parodic image of the Virgin. This ritualistic subversion of hierarchy and orthodoxy is a visually powerful and historically detailed dramatisation of those medieval festivals of misrule conjecturally derived from the saturnalian rituals of Rome. An appropriate source is provided by the well-known description by a Parisian academic writing in 1445:

> Who, I ask you, with any Christian feelings, will not condemn when priests and clerks are seen wearing masks and monstrous visages at the hours of Office: dancing in the choir, dressed as women, panders or minstrels, singing lewd songs? They eat black-pudding at the horn of the altar next the celebrant, play at dice there, censing with foul smoke from the soles of old shoes, and running and leaping about the whole church in unblushing, shameless iniquity; and then, finally, they are seen driving about the town and its theatres in carts and deplorable carriages to make an infamous spectacle for the laughter of bystanders and partici-pants, with indecent gestures of the body and language most unchaste and scurrilous.[10]

The elements of parody and subversion, the substitution of licence for restraint, obscenity for virtue, the origiastic celebra-tion of the material body for the metaphysical rituals of the Mass, are here correctly identified as a form of drama – an 'infamous spectacle' for the entertainment of bystanders. Carnival is not simply release or escape from restraint and discipline: it is a tem-porary period of sanctioned licence, in which a permitted over-throw of established hierarchy is enacted through parodic rituals which do not, despite their appearance of anarchy and liberation, escape from the formal character of ritual. The medieval church allowed such temporary suspensions of order, just as Rome per-mitted its slaves their day of privilege and supremacy, not from any commitment to liberty and popular rule, but as a means of channelling subversive energy into acceptable and assimilable forms.[11]

By jettisoning the Sly-frame Zeffirelli may in the opinion of some observers have been indicating his contempt for his 'original'. But unlike Jonathan Miller's television version, which omitted the 'Induction' altogether, or the same director's subse-quent RSC production (which simply replaced the 'Induction' with musical interludes performed by some pointlessly happy *commedia dell'arte* morris dancers) Zeffirelli has sought and found an alternative establishing context which is at once an educated and intelligent historical reconstruction and a brilliant initial exposé of the production's principles of interpretation. Jack Jorgens has effectively analysed the relationship between induction and denouement:

> This rowdy procession with its chaos of shouts, songs, and shrieks of laughter disrupts the daily routine of Padua, routs seriousness and pretensions to dignity, overturns the hierarchies of power, and dissolves boredom and drudgery. It challenges the populace, tests their sexual prowess, creative energy, thirst, appetites, and late-night endurance. It renews communal feelings by replacing social and economic competition with an orgy of hospitality. Part of the idyll is that modern urban paranoia is banished and creative anarchy reigns, cementing the society together and making life – fraught as it is with failure, sickness and death – more tolerable.
> (Jorgens, *Shakespeare and Film*, pp. 74-5)

The function of carnival is to promote social integration: the purpose of ritualised disorder to endorse the stability of the order that can afford to permit its own temporary abolition. Such a model of contradiction resolved may well serve as an appropriate pattern for Shakespeare's comedy: Kate's subversive energy of resistance and Petruchio's parodic exposure of commercialised relationship both serve ultimately, and paradoxically, to reintegrate the disrupted order of Paduan society; just as the drama that contained and enacted this reintegration function as an endorsement of the imposed 'order' of the Tudor state. Zeffirelli's 'Induction' also became, by virtue of the circumstances of its first exhibition, in a sense, self-reflexive: since this boisterous display of Bohemian anarchy and anti-social energy was enacted, like the old festivals of misrule, before representatives of the very authority whose power such rituals are designed to challenge – in this case, the British monarchy.

According to Zeffirelli's aesthetic, the sets displayed realism to the
last detail. When [John] Stride approached the stage on opening
night to get a feel of the sets and lighting, he discovered Zeffirelli
flicking a brush with dirty, watery paint about eighteen inches
above the floor. 'This is where the dogs pee on the walls', the director explained. Then he flicked a little higher, saying, 'and this is
where the men pee'. (Levenson, *Romeo and Juliet*, p. 100)

This anecdote, recalled from the 1960 Old Vic production of
Romeo and Juliet, displays several characteristics of Zeffirelli as
director/designer: his personal intervention into the labour of the
design process; his naturalistic concern with accuracy and fidelity
of representation and his excessively punctilious eye for detail.
His links with naturalist conventions colour all his theatrical and
film work, both in terms of directing and designing. As we have
seen, his '*cine-verité* documentary on Renaissance Verona' cast as
principals actors whose youthfulness and inexperience would
help to dissolve their personalities into those of the tragic lovers;
and as we shall see below, similar motives underlay the casting of
Burton and Taylor in the *Shrew*.

But what exactly constitutes naturalism in terms of movie
design? Zeffirelli's sets for the 1960 *Romeo and Juliet* were easily
recognisable as a familiar formulation of theatrical conventions,
deriving ultimately from the pictorial perspective stages of the
nineteenth-century theatre. Naturalism in the cinema was associated, certainly in Zeffirelli's immediate cultural context, with the
location shooting and sharp black-and-white photography of
films like de Sica's *Bicycle Thieves*, the cinematic equivalent of
Zola's scientific novel. The filmic naturalism of Zeffirelli's movies
has much more in common with the highly coloured and decorative realism of Visconti's historical films, where realism has taken
on the glowing tints of historical painting rather than the stark
monochrome of documentary film. It is this historical realism,
framed always by the pervasive influences of visual art, that

constitutes the primary medium of *The Taming of the Shrew*. *Romeo and Juliet* was filmed in a wide variety of locations throughout Italy, since Zeffirelli wanted to fill his screen with the concrete reality of Renaissance city streets, churches and palaces, wooded hillsides and romantic balconies.[12] The *Shrew* was filmed entirely in the de Laurentiis studios in Rome.

As far as Zeffirelli is concerned, a director is responsible also for design: and possibly his training as an artist made it inevitable that he should visualise a production with a painter's eye. That visualisation was not simply a matter of reconstructing an accurate realistic background (down to the dog-pee on the walls) before which the action could be played: it seems to be much more a question of the director-designer's artistic sensibility evoking a design concept from his own reading of the text.

> Although he deliberately adopted this older realist aesthetic – he found it imaginatively stimulating (*The Times*, 19 September 1960) – Zeffirelli also relied on instinct and fantasy. He analysed musical or dramatic texts into images, which he composed in a synthesis determined not only by his understanding, but also by his emotional response to the work. Like the young Peter Brook, Zeffirelli believed in 'a controlling image, a core'. His image always took visual form, or a painterly design. In a conversation with Laurence Kitchin on the BBC, 11 February 1964, Zeffirelli described the emergence of this image as 'a creative beginning', the sole creative moment for the artist interpreting his subject or the director interpreting his script. What comes after the visualisation simply elaborates it; and in stage design, what follows may involve collaboration with the author.
>
> For Zeffirelli, the stage became a huge canvas on which to produce the impression of a living fresco with paint, fabric, colour, timber. (Levenson, *Romeo and Juliet*, pp. 86-7)

Although the studio sets designed to represent Renaissance Padua were insistently naturalistic – 'Mongiardino's magnificent sets were so perfect that even rainstorms could be reproduced, with the water running downhill, without the cobbled streets of

"Padua" looking any the worse for wear' (Lane, *Films and Filming*, p. 52) – the overwhelming emphasis was on a pictorial evocation of Renaissance culture, a colourful and chaotic genre painting which could be galvanised into vitality by the nervous mobility and fluidity of *ciné-verité* camera-work. On the set John Francis Lane discovered cameraman Ossie Morris 'holding a well-thumbed book of Correggio reproductions as he studied the lighting for a shot', and actors 'busily studying books about Venetian art' (Lane, *Films and Filming*, p. 51). Reviewers responded to this 'painterly' quality, often with cross-references, appreciative or critical, to the visual arts:

> The picture is enticing to look at, with a sunny-natured opening scene in a gauzy drizzle, high shots of rapt onlookers and crankily angled passages, brownish tints through the reds, and Burton in a bucolic make-up that looks like a Venetian portrait ... [13]
>
> Richard Burton ... bearded and looking like Henry VIII in a Holbein ... caught in soft colours with a yellowish tint which suggests a Renaissance painting under old varnish: and while no particular master seems to supply the models, there is a blowzy blonde courtesan on view who has stepped straight out of a Bellini.[14]
>
> The film has been filtered through a sort of burnt sienna light that gives it the muted golden haze of many Renaissance paintings, and is indeed lovely to look at, but as a series of stills, not moving pictures.[15]

The tension disclosed here between pictorial 'naturalism' (designed to absorb the characters into a convincing reconstruction of historical reality), and what might more accurately be termed a 'picturesque' style, achieved by systematic quoting of well-known visual sources (which actually draws the spectator's attention to its own patently displayed artifice) constitutes a problem of interpretation both for this film and for Jonathan Miller's television version. The tradition of pictorial setting derives, through the intermediary of silent film, from a theatre of historical realism: its functions are ordinarily naturalistic, as exemplified by, for instance, the historical films of Luchino Visconti (e.g. *The Leopard*); and certainly by Miller's BBC *Shrew*. But there is a point at which a pictorial setting comes 'into view' in its own right, when it ceases to provide naturalistic camouflage for the figures within its frame, and becomes self-reflexive, the object of its own narcissistic gaze. Jack Jorgens feels that this style of visual design is in Zeffirelli's *Shrew* so pervasive as to deprive the film of any pretensions to realism:

> Zeffirelli has little use for the realism in the play ... There are touches of vivid realistic detail in the film ... but these are used for comic effect, and work to heighten the colourful, rich portrait of Renaissance Italy. From the opening moments when Lucentio and Tranio, riding in a gentle rain, spy Padua haloed with a rainbow beyond a pastoral vision with shepherds, sheep, and greenery, the film is a beautiful idyll bathed in gold-coloured light. (Jorgens, pp. 70-1)

Tori Haring-Smith takes the argument a stage further: for her the film is not merely in appearance artificial; it is self-consciously concerned to exhibit its own artifice, and to use its picturesqueness as a framing device capable of the same distancing effects as the play's Christopher Sly framework:

> Although he did not include Shakespeare's 'Induction', Franco Zeffirelli achieved a similar blending of reality and artificiality ... using studio realism, shading, and Panavision to keep the viewer constantly aware that the film is and is not real. Since Zeffirelli did not have the physical arrangement of a theatre to establish the metaphor of reality and illusion, he could not rely on the 'Induction' to introduce that theme. Instead, the film begins with an enormous painting of the Italian countryside. Although the picture fills the screen and the frame is not visible, the landscape is obviously unreal ... The 'real' world we view is always framed or enclosed in this way by the painted landscape.[16]

It is my view that these visual conventions do not in themselves contain clear and definitive statements of their own significance: the meanings they make available depend largely on an interdependence with the other signifying codes of the production. Thus broadly similar design conventions, coupled with very different approaches to genre, style, and acting method, produce in Zeffirelli's film and Jonathan Miller's TV productions, very dissimilar and indeed incommensurable dramatic worlds.

Within Zeffirelli's visual context of painterly composition, the principal generic emphasis is on farce. 'Zeffirelli turns the taming of Elizabeth Taylor's shrew by Richard Burton's ribald Petruchio into an assault course conducted with the comic complications of an obstacle race.'[17] Farce is primarily of course a visual genre, depending on movement, incongruous juxtaposition, interruption, rapid reversal and Zeffirelli makes full use of farce's principal structural motif, the chase. But farce is hardly calculated to complement or enable the careful construction of picturesque tableaux that immediately evoke the visual sources they are derived from. On the contrary, the incessant chaotic mobility of farce is likely to upset the visual stability and spatial configuration of any picturesque set. The tension between these apparently incompatible elements led critics such as David Robinson to complain about Zeffirelli's continual disturbance of the celluloid canvas:

> The first shots of Lucentio and Tranio riding out of one of those zig-zag back-drops from the Quattrocento masters and wearing, with pleasant inconsequence, clothes that seem to come from the Triumph of Maximillian, is enchanting. And the design throughout betrays a similar care. But it is largely negated by Zeffirelli's quite surprising ineptitude in composing groupings on the screen. Again and again the extravagant hurly-burlies of activity into which he launches extras and principals alike ,,, are as ugly as they are extravagantly busy.[18]

Other critics argued that the elaborate minutiae of naturalistic detail and the violent turbulence of rapid physical motion simply trip over one another and reduce the visual composition to chaos:

The intention to beguile the eye with swirling movement breaks down because so much is perpetually going on that the eventual effect is simply fussy. Dogs run about incessantly, characters hurl artefacts either to the floor or at each other; the entire cast at frequent intervals breaks into hearty communal applause or rowdy communal laughter. People fall about, or swing, Tarzan-like, on ropes; or run pointlessly after one another across roofs. After a couple of reels of this, the spectator's dearest wish is that everyone would stand still and shut up. (Roud, *Guardian*, 3 March 1967)

The necessary reliance of farce on physical objects – doors, windows, beds, projectiles – certainly links the genre to a primarily visual, pictorial mode of presentation. Jorgens provides a brief catalogue of objects which figure in the film's physical language of 'festive destructiveness':

Kate smashes shutters and stained-glass windows, splinters music stands and lutes, rips out the bell rope which Petruchio tugs upon so daintily, and tears loose a railing to hurl at him. Petruchio drunkenly knocks over wine glasses and pulls down curtains at Hortensio's house, smashes through railings and brick walls, and falls through the roof in Baptista's barn. He pummels and spits upon his servants, bisects a hat with a family sword causing the haberdasher to faint, tears dresses, hurls food, overturns the dinner table, and makes a shambles of the wedding bed. (Jorgens, *Shakespeare and Film*, pp. 71-2)

But these are all objects in motion, things thrown into continual kinaesthesia by the incessant physical activity of farce; they are not the scrupulously arranged and beautifully lit property details of a cinematic still-life portrait. Similar tendencies towards pictorial effect in Jonathan Miller's BBC production, accompanied as they are by a predominantly naturalistic approach to acting, are actually much more successful in constructing static, elaborately framed visual compositions. The result is that the entire design concept of the production can be assimilated firmly into the nineteenth-century traditions of pictorial staging. Zeffirelli's style is much more flexible and self-deconstructing: his film with its elaborate historical and geographical setting, points even more formally towards the visual sources quoted, and yet is prepared to scatter the spatial configurations thus achieved into a turbulent mêlée of violent visual motion. No physical background, however carefully ordered and lovingly constructed, is permitted to overshadow or subdue the spontaneous physical energies of this farcical dramatic action.

An inexhaustibly inventive and subversive approach to its own formal devices is entirely in keeping with that spirit of carnival established from the outset in Zeffirelli's substituted 'Induction'. There we see the formal rituals of religion subjected to parody and inversion and the film throughout adopts a comparably subversive perspective on the classic drama it is self-consciously mediating. The rhythms, actions, gestures and grimaces of farce continually recall Sam Taylor's 1929 (Pickford/Fairbanks) film production, the classic Hollywood 'vulgarisation' of Shakespeare and there are even echoes of the musical *Kiss me Kate*. Some of the most obvious visual devices are parodic rather than representational in effect: reviewers unanimously noted the Burton/Henry VIII visual parallel, but traced it to its distant source in Holbein rather than to a more immediate analogue – Charles Laughton's comic portrayal of Henry VIII in Alexander Korda's *The Private Life of Henry VIII* (1933), of which Burton's performance is a direct parody. In general this self-reflexive quality of the film has up to now remained underrated or even unnoticed, though it is at certain points obvious enough – in one scene Petruchio and Grumio combine in a bawling song which actually joins in with the musical soundtrack!

It was by electing to subordinate naturalism, psychology, scholarly respect for the classical virtues and sober moral earnestness, to a sustained activation of rombustious high-jinks that Zeffirelli reaped the particular condemnation of those critics who felt that the play was being distorted, abused and wrenched from its natural and original character. The director's reliance on visual effects, whether of decor, setting or action, was felt by many observers to represent an unjustifiable sacrifice of Shakespeare's predominantly verbal dramatic medium.

Paul Dehn, Suso Ceccho d'Amico and Zeffirelli himself, whose screenplay credit could be for dialogue reduction, skittishly recognised their debt to 'William Shakespeare, without whom they would have been at a loss for words'.

This credit really sets the tone of the film: an indefatigable hammering playfulness which more or less assumes that no one will be paying much attention to those words they are never at a loss for.[19]

Zeffirelli's approach to the problem ... of understanding Shakespeare's language has seemed to be ... to distract the audience from the words as much as possible. Sometimes you feel (wrongly I am sure) a positive contempt for the text in the lengths Zeffirelli will go to stage diversions to take your mind off it. (Robinson, *Financial Times*, 3 March 1967)

The real trouble is, quite simply, that Shakespeare's high-spirited baby has been thrown out with the Zeffirelli bathwater.

The director seems to have had no faith in his material, and an almost narcissistic affection for his own cleverness.

So he has imposed chases, horseplay, slapstick, belches, false beards, carnival noses, priest-baiting, crashes through walls and roofs.[20]

... Zeffirelli's aim seems to be to elicit from his audience an active contempt for the words. Visual extravagance is the keynote ... [21]

Shakespeare's text has been drastically cut, which wouldn't have been bothersome (the play is hardly one of his masterpieces) if director Franco Zeffirelli had found less oafish ways of 'opening up' the play. It seems that for most of this long movie roofs are falling in, tables of food overturning, ladies wallowing in mud. The wit and tension in the dialogues between Petruchio and Katherina are lost because Zeffirelli has them running an obstacle course while they bicker – this is to make the material cinematic, in case someone misses the point (Farber, *Film Quarterly*, p. 61).

I have quoted this line of hostile criticism so extensively in order to illustrate its extraordinary uniformity of tone. Such bilious reactions should be juxtaposed against Jack Jorgen's sensitive and intelligent analysis of the *purpose* and *function* of farcical business and conventions within the overall structure of the film, and with my own discussion of the complex and subtle uses of visual design. To criticise farce for being farcical is simply an absurd procedure; to contrast a version of Shakespeare unfavourably with some ideal model (which is never defined) carries very little weight as argument and is designed only to elicit from the reader a visceral response of conformity: we do not pretend to understand the ineffable mystery of Shakespeare but we are confident that whatever that transcendent essence may be, this is not it. Extensive cutting of the text, the dramatisation of reported scenes such as the wedding, the substitution of visual images for verbal effects, are equally characteristic of Olivier's *Henry V*: but we would not find in commentary and criticism on that film the same accents of outraged bardolatry. Akira Kurosawa makes films of Shakespeare without using the text: they are regarded as masterpieces of cinematic interpretation.

It seems to be generally accepted that a film of Shakespeare cannot *be* 'Shakespeare': in the sense that while a theatrical performance may aspire to reactivate with some fidelity verbal and dramatic structures which were composed for a theatre, a movie has no choice but to adapt and radically interpret the material to a specifically cinematic form. It is far more productive, if that premise be accepted, to compare a film of a Shakespeare play with other film versions of Shakespeare, with other films from the repertory of the same *auteur*, with films from a comparable genre. To evaluate a film version against a conception of its 'original' is, since Shakespeare did not make films, a meaningless procedure.

Both the director and those who have worked with him speak of Zeffirelli 's technique as a very free and open collaboration with the actor.

He has a highly unselfish imagination for other people. He once said, 'You can't force an actor. He doesn't play with his technique, he plays with his own human qualities. My job is to offer many different solutions to him, and then to choose the right one. It may be comic or tragic, but it must be the right one *for him*.'[22]

[John] Stride remembers, 'he never worked from any book. His theory was improvisation within a framework. We were never made to stick exactly to the same mode ... Nobody wrote down the actor's moves ... because they were never the same two nights running – there was no blocking. (quoted in Levenson, *Romeo and Juliet*, p. 92)

Yet nothing, surely, could be further from an open-ended experimental approach than the casting of Burton and Taylor as Petruchio and Katherina. Zeffirelli referred to that choice as something natural, inevitable, self-evident: 'Of course we thought of Burton and Taylor immediately' (*Evening Standard*, 5 July 1965). The Burtons, as a highly public and publicity-conscious screen couple, were in the habit of presenting to the media an image of domestic life similar to the relationship of Katherina and Petruchio. This may well have been an elaborately constructed fantasy for media consumption, but it represents an overtly displayed persona which blended easily into the principal roles of the *Shrew*, as it had in the previous year underpinned the laceratingly conflictual relationship in *Who's Afraid of Virginia Woolf*:

The Taming of the Shrew, or the son of *Virginia Woolf*, can be best understood as cashing in on last year's success; people will apparently never tire of peeping in on a fantasy version of the Burtons' home life. (Farber, *Film Quarterly*, p. 61)

Once again Elizabeth Taylor and Richard Burton clash head-on in a riot of verbal and visual fights and frolic.

Once again they prove that theirs is certainly an explosive and often a deeply rewarding film partnership.[23]

The movie is a news event – another colourful episode in the lives of Elizabeth Taylor and Richard Burton, whose supposed follies happen to fit into a comedy from the First Folio. Burton's

Petruchio is a ringer for Henry VIII, played with broad and boozy licence. Elizabeth's Kate is a bosom heaving with feminist wiles rather than congenital bad temper. She clearly adores the brute and lets him tame her just to prolong the fun.[24]

If it is reasonable to entertain a suspicion that the principal players were cast as much for their off-screen public personalities as for their dramatic appropriateness, there would seem to be little scope for a director to promote experiment and openness. Commenting on the theatrical personalities of Burton and Taylor, Zeffirelli's philosophy of acting began to appear remarkably diluted and enfeebled:

> She's a marvellous girl. So unpredictable. She's not a set personality. You don't know everything about her and this is very exciting for a director – and it might be a problem too. You feel she has not given her best yet.
>
> Even Richard, who is a man who has done everything, has still to give his best in the movies. The best is still to come. I think they're both in progress.
>
> They're both open. I've had to be open in my own work in the past few years and always gambled. This is what we'll do with the film. There's a danger of disaster – but we'll take great pleasure in what we do. (quoted in *Evening Standard*, 5 July 1965)

Uncertain whether he is talking about Burton and Taylor or Antony and Cleopatra, Zeffirelli here is trying to make a transparent piece of type-casting sound like open-ended avant-garde experimentation.

Whether this linking of off-screen and on-screen roles was part of the director's intention or not, the massively over-exposed public personalities of the two stars inevitably coloured their participation in the film. Petruchio, for example, inherits from the Shakespearean 'Induction' the drunkenness of Christopher Sly: he appears constantly intoxicated and at his wedding so drunk as to fall asleep during the service, waking only to gulp the communion wine with an oath. Film-viewers would not however associate the hero's drunkenness with the lost 'Induction', but with the much-publicised drunken exploits of Richard Burton, who found unlimited justification in his own cultural style – product of the Welsh mining valleys, angry young man, Bohemian artist as a young dog – for being ostentatiously drunk at every available opportunity. This aspect of the film now, after Burton's death from alcohol-related illness, evokes a mingled sense of bitter irony and lacerating pathos. Similarly, no amount of shrill vituperation, aggressive hysteria and volatile temper can disguise Elizabeth Taylor's startling physical beauty. Above all, Katherina and Petruchio are the Burton-Taylor couple – rowing and fighting, divorcing and remarrying, but always in love and always to be reunited – before they actually appear in character on the screen.

It seems therefore merely appropriate and natural that Katherina and Petruchio should, whatever their initial predispositions as mercenary fortune-hunter and mutinous virago, and in despite of the aggression and hostility enacted between them, be in love, at first sight, and in all probability happily (if noisily) ever after.

> A routine that was merely brutal – can it have even pleased its patriarchal first-night audience? – has been thawed out into a sexy light comedy. Zeffirelli is one up on the Bard by letting Petruchio and Kate fancy each other from the word go. The light of appetite, kindling in the eyes of both, suggests that the hostilities have at least some end in view. What Zeffirelli has done is to humanise Shakespeare's dreary mechanics, and turn a Punch-and-Judy show into a species of love story.[25]

The 'love-at-first-sight' motif is rendered conspicuous in the film by looks and gestures, and subsequently reinforced by Kate's silent complicity in Petruchio's announcement of their wedding, and her loyal pursuit of him to his house when he abandons her at the gates of Padua.

The 'taming' plot is thus drained of the various historical and moral significances attributed to it: its long denouement necessarily has to be translated into the terms of farce, since it has become purely a game, a mutual compact of reciprocal entertainment. Underlying the mechanical surface action we infer the presence of sexual attraction, mutual admiration and a genial and sensitive human nature. 'Richard Burton is Shakespeare's Petruchio all right: an adventurer, a self-satisfied bully, but with a touch of redeeming gaiety; and Mr Burton has a pretty moment at the end when his face betrays anxiety lest Kate should not obey his commands – and relief when she does.'[26]

These touches of 'redeeming' humanity are of course the result of actor's intervention and of directorial decision, and cannot be authenticated by reference back to Shakespeare's intentions: they are the strategies of interpretation that in all performances mediate the Elizabethan text to a contemporary audience. Elizabeth Taylor's Katherina expressed to most viewers nothing unpleasant or unattractive in her shrewishness. 'Elizabeth Taylor, her shapely bosom swelling with fury out of almost topless dresses, gives a tremendous performance as the delightful but spiteful Katherina. What a ball of fire she is, as she stands, with hands on hips, eyes blazing, leaning forward as she spits out insults like an angry swan'.[27] It is not necessary to have been insulted by a swan to recognise the accuracy of this comment: what the actress communicates is a fierce energy of sexual attraction, not a sullen force of hostile resistance.

Katherina's final speech of surrender articulates a resignation to Petruchio and to marriage; and an ironical self-consciousness calculated to suggest that the transparent accents of obedient orthodoxy belie the true vitality and sexual energy of their turbulent relationship. The first element is foregrounded by showing Kate looking in an obviously 'broody' way at some children, playing with dogs before the banquet table; and the second by displaying her immediate and passionate surrender to Petruchio's 'come kiss me, Kate'; and by having her sneak quietly out so that Petruchio has to commence the chase all over again.

Such a predominant emphasis on the central roles of the *Shrew*, with the additional reinforcement of the Burton-Taylor personality cult, inevitably left little space for any coherent or considered development of the Bianca-plot which, as many critics complained, is hardly present in the film at all.

> The film's roster of delightful performers puts up a commendable struggle against the total submersion which afflicts both plot and sub-plot.[28]

> I've no doubt that Shakespeare purists will be cross to find the Lucentio-Bianca story reduced to a sketchy outline, lots of speeches cut short and several characters missing altogether.[29]

> Zeffirelli shows himself aware that the text is still playable as it stands. His film is nearly brave, and with most of the cast he assembled, could have been tremendous: performers like Cyril Cusack (Grumio), Victor Spinetti (Hortensio, a role cut to ribbons), Michael Hordern as the shrew's father, and the young sub-plot lovers, Michael York and Natasha Pyne, could have given far more, given in turn their chance. But all is subordinated to the big, boisterous and box-office flyting of Mr Burton and Elizabeth Taylor's Kate.[30]

These comments are in no way unfair descriptions of the film's marginalisation of the Bianca-plot: a typical moment is that in which an entire scene of courtship between Lucentio and Bianca is subordinated to an extra-textual chase, Petruchio pursuing Kate around the dumbstruck lovers and out on to the rooftops. The rarified air of comic courtly love appears to stifle the boisterous energies of Petruchio and Katherina, and the film too elbows both characters and atmosphere of the sub-plot aside to escape into a more vigorous air. What little detail of the sub-plot remains in the film serves two purposes: to contrast the conventional romantic relationship of Bianca and Lucentio with the bizarre and violent wooing rituals of Petruchio and Katherina; and to juxtapose the abrasive vitality and bracing energy of Petruchio against figures of pathetic ineffectualness like Victor Spinetti's camp Hortensio, or Michael Hordern's brilliant self-parody as the synthesis of all the senescent patriarchs he has ever played.

By infusing the play with visual and musical overtones of romance; insisting on the reciprocal passion of tamer and tamed; translating the violence of the play into a medium of farce, where destruction is always innocuous; and by casting the end-result of these operations into the form of a film, Zeffirelli has altered the rules of the game to such an extent that the film has little to say about the sexual politics of *The Taming of the Shrew*. The transformation of play into film is so complete that the historical roots of the Shakespearean text are scarcely any longer visible to provide the viewer with any specific structure of orientation. The sexual politics of the film can only therefore be interpreted and evaluated in terms of its own cultural context and historical moment: and I would argue that in this respect Zeffirelli's film is not so much anti-feminist as a-feminist.

Since the farce genre of the film, in its preoccupation with physical capacities such as running, throwing, swinging, balancing, shouting, fighting – assumes a mutual equality and reciprocal balance of forces between the sexes, it simply does not address the questions of family and marriage in any way that would prove interesting or useful to a feminist cultural politics. Zeffirelli's version of the *Shrew* actually substitutes, for the structural antithesis of the sexes in Shakespeare's play, a new distinction; between the sterile, hypocritical and mercenary society of Padua, and the irrepressible and unassimilable energy of two Bohemian anarchists. Both Katherina and Petruchio are initially, in their different ways, at odds with conventional society and in their fortuitous collision both find the possibility of a common cause.

> … the taming is not the heart of the film. Rather, it is the good-natured but thorough assault of Kate and Petruchio on Padua and Paduan values. Zeffirelli turns loose two rebels against hypocrites, greedy pantaloons, time-servers, blind idealists, tricky maidens, and crafty widows. They declare war on respectability, duty, religion, sighing literary romance, and narrow materialism. (Jorgens, *Shakespeare and Film*, p. 72)

CHAPTER SEVEN

Romeo and Juliet (1991)

ॐ

R OMEO AND JULIET is a book that can be read, a text that can be interpreted and a play that can be performed. These differing manifestations of *Romeo and Juliet* may all be regarded as aspects of the same 'thing': a play-script written by Shakespeare some time in the 1590s; a performance-text that was popular in the Renaissance theatre, and has remained in the theatrical repertory every since; and a readable text that is still widely appreciated, studied and enjoyed, not least within the framework of the contemporary Literature syllabus.

We call all these cultural products 'Shakespeare's *Romeo and Juliet*'. Yet whichever of these forms we look at, we are likely to encounter not a solid ground of common responses to a uniform object: but on the contrary, great variety in readings, sharp divergences of interpretation in critical analysis, and wide liberty of interpretation in theatrical production. This chapter is not so much an attempt to establish and demonstrate what *Romeo and Juliet* is, as an effort to describe and analyse the number of things it is capable of becoming when activated by the imagination of readers, motivated by the argument and debate of critics, and reconstructed in performance by the interpretative strategies of stage directors, film producers and actors.

Yet we begin with a powerful conviction that Shakespeare's

Romeo and Juliet is a simple, identifiable cultural artefact. We also feel at the same time that it is (paradoxically) complex enough to contain all this imaginative, critical and interpretative activity, some of which seems so varied and free-ranging as to throw the play's uniform identity into question. But from a common sense point of view, we assume the presence of a straightforward narrative and dramatic construction, which remains always in any of its manifestations 'Shakespeare's *Romeo and Juliet*'. After all, the play's basic 'story' seems both simple, treating of common experience, and unconnected to specific circumstances of time and place and history.

What could be more fundamental and enduring than a story about young love, sudden and passionate and all-embracing, threatened and pushed towards its tragic destiny by a range of external forces, working in unintentional but fatal conspiracy? What could be truer to our sense of the universality of experience, than a narrative which shows these young lovers locked in conflict with parents and peers, cherishing the uniqueness of their passion, and trying unsuccessfully to integrate it with a hostile and authoritarian adult world? The basic 'story' of the play, considered as something independent of Shakespeare's drama, seems almost archetypal in its symbolic centrality, almost mythical in its timeless romance and enduring relevance. The basic situation, of two lovers kept apart by parental control and family conflict, inspired by their love to cross boundaries of social division in a symbolic union which entails tragic consequences, could be (and has been) adapted to fit many historical situations apart from the one used by Shakespeare. The Leonard Bernstein/ Stephen Sondheim musical *West Side Story*[1] started with Shakespeare, but was able to move the central action of the story into a completely different cultural situation, where racial hostility between ethnic groups in New York replaces the family vendetta of Shakespeare's Renaissance Italy. Was that operation possible because *Romeo and Juliet* is an archetypal narrative of fundamental and permanent human experience?

We would expect a story of young love thwarted to appeal continually to young people themselves, by offering the dramatic representation of a familiar predicament with which it is easy for them to identify. Love is experienced in *Romeo and Juliet* as an immediate and absolute demand, with which there is no possibility of compromise; circumstances force that love underground into secrecy and concealment; the emotion itself seems incommunicable to other people, most of whom in turn (whether intentionally or not) treat the lovers and their relationship with indifference or hostility; and throughout the play we see both Romeo and Juliet subjected to impossible or unsympathetic parental demands, bullied by members of their own generation and unable to express their emotions freely except to one another. So in terms of experience, *Romeo and Juliet* seems a story calculated to appeal directly to young people, and by virtue of its crystallisation of an unchanging human reality, to all other readers or spectators of Shakespeare.

If we accept that *Romeo and Juliet* deals with a common if not 'universal' experience of love and enforced separation, exactly how 'universal' is the particular chain of events dramatised in Shakespeare's theatrical narrative? We can approach this question by being more precise about the forces in the play that challenge the relationship of Romeo and Juliet. Why are the young lovers unable simply to follow their inclination and be together? There are in actuality two forces of separation, intimately connected with each other: 'family' and 'feud'. Romeo and Juliet cannot marry or even 'go out' together because one is a Montague and the other a Capulet, and because they are young. Their family dependence (neither can marry openly without their parents' consent) means that they are subject to the authority of their parents and therefore to family loyalties and enmities. This situation precipitates open dramatic conflicts – such as Juliet's resistance to the arranged marriage with Paris – between the adult heads of the family and the younger generation, which certainly seem like archetypally familiar domestic difficulties. But while we think of the basic conflict as one *within* the family, between generations, this particular story belongs to a context where loyalty to a family entails, whatever the misgivings or reservations of the individual, a duty of opposition to another family. It is on account of the long-standing feud between the two houses of Capulets and Montague that Juliet's parents are assumed to be inevitably hostile to the idea of a 'mixed marriage'. We do not see Romeo involved in internal family conflicts in the same way as Juliet: his parents do not even appear between the first scene and the third act of the play, and Romeo is more preoccupied with the hostility of the Capulets than with the resistance of his parents. This may be nothing more than an inequality of freedom between men and women in this society: but Romeo certainly does not confide in his parents, and we can assume that, like the Capulet parents, they too would feel a natural hostility towards a love that transgresses the dividing line between the families.

Are we still dealing, in this story of a love that grows in the no man's land between two families at war with one another, with a 'universal' context? Clearly there are many circumstances in which relationships can be poisoned or destroyed by situations of racial hostility, ethnic enmity or class division. We could easily see in such contexts – the middle-class family disapproving of their daughter's working-class boyfriend, the Jewish family trying to forbid their son's marriage to a non-Jew – typical 'Romeo and Juliet' situations. More pointedly, circumstances of open and violent conflict between countries, races or political groups – between, say, a colonised nation and an imperialist power – could readily bring a simple heterosexual coupling into conflict with family and community loyalties. Joan Lingard's novel *Across the Barricades* does exactly that.[2] It sets a version of *Romeo and Juliet* in Northern Ireland.

The pervasive presence throughout the world of violent conflict and deep-rooted enmity will ensure a plentiful supply of analogous situations, where a simple relationship of love may cut across other binding obligations. Furthermore, the co-existence within British society of different ethnic groups with varying attitudes towards matters of sex and marriage can put us in closer touch with even some of the more 'archaic' aspects of the Romeo and Juliet story: an Asian girl expected by her parents to comply with an arranged marriage would certainly find Juliet's situation understandable. But do these factors make this particular play an expression of universal experience?

If we look again at the two forces which operate within the play's narrative and dramatic structure to prise and keep the two lovers apart – 'family' and 'feud' – we begin to see that this quality of 'universality' may be more apparent than real. In Shakespeare's play 'family' and 'feud' are linked and interdependent terms in the structural conflict. There is, we could say, a 'vertical' dimension of conflict, that which takes place between two generations within a single family, between old and young. But there is also an additional 'horizontal' dimension, the conflict *between* families that is rooted in the Montague-Capulet feud. This horizontal cross-family conflict has to be linked up with the vertical internal family conflicts before the conditions of a 'Romeo and Juliet' story can be fully realised.

Within each of these two separate spheres of conflict, we can feel that we are confronted by an apparently 'universal' quality of experience. When we see Juliet being forced by her parents to accept marriage to a man she does not love, we can feel confident that the conflict is taking place within that vertical dimension of internal family conflict, and that it is an experience by no means peculiar to Shakespeare's England or Renaissance Verona. If we regard the feud as a symbolic representation of social division, then that too can seem depressingly universal. There are always social groups divided against one another, with varying degrees of intensity from ingrained prejudice and mutual dislike to violent civil war. But the story of Romeo and Juliet cannot 'come together' as a narrative structure until *both these dimensions of conflict* (vertical and horizontal, inter-family and intra-family) *are linked with one another* into a single unified narrative and dramatic action.

At this point the structural pattern formed by the narrative starts to look more unique and specific, and (though composed of universal-seeming elements) not universal in itself. We all at one stage or another of our lives can find ourselves in opposition to our parents: but not all our families are locked into a violent conflict with another family group. We could all think of examples of societies bitterly divided by factional conflict: but that conflict need not be reproduced *within* each group by a conflict between the generations – in fact, the very opposite is often the case, where families are internally united by the very strife that divides them against others.

West Side Story is recognised as an adaptation of *Romeo and Juliet*. By 'adaptation' we would normally understand a version of the story which did not simply reproduce Shakespeare's text and Shakespeare's words, but developed the basic story into a more or less different treatment: transferring the action to a different time and place; substituting a modern script or screenplay for the Elizabethan text; translating the play into a new form, such as the popular musical. An adaptation, we might say, is formed by composing variations on a theme. But the 'theme' on which *West Side Story* plays variations is not precisely the story of *Romeo and Juliet* as I have just defined it. In *West Side Story*, the feud between rival New York street-gangs is conducted entirely by young people. The leading figures on each side are young men: Bernardo, brother of Maria (Juliet), and the equivalent of Tybalt in Shakespeare's play, heads the gang of Puerto Rican 'Sharks'; while Riff (who like Mercutio in Shakespeare's play is killed in a brawl as a consequence of intervention by Tony/Romeo) leads the white gang of 'Jets'. The respective *parents* of Tony and Maria are effectively excluded from the musical play. The lovers refer to them, but they never appear, except when as an off-stage, off-screen voice Maria's mother calls her indoors during the film's equivalent of the 'balcony-scene'.

The structural pattern in *West Side Story* contains two generations but they are not evenly divided, whites and Puerto Ricans, Capulet and Montague, as they are in Shakespeare's play. The conflict is between groups of young people who face one another across a bitter divide of racial hostility. The adult characters in the musical all stand outside the gang-warfare and attempt to stop it. Doc (Tony's employer and the equivalent of Friar Laurence) tries to reason with the gangs; the policemen Officer Krupke and Lieutenant Schrank try to stop their fighting by a mixture of persuasion and force; a well-meaning but hapless youth-club leader (comically named Glad Hand) tries ineffectually to unite the gangs at a dance (Shakespeare's Capulet ball). The role of Juliet's Nurse, who of course tended Juliet as a baby, is fulfilled by Anita, Bernardo's girl friend, who seems not much older than Maria herself.

Now although this pattern has its basis in *Romeo and Juliet* (so that certain figures, such as Friar Laurence and Tybalt, can be more or less accurately reproduced) it does not imitate the play's narrative and dramatic structure, but produces another, different one, concerned with teenage violence, not with an old-established feud between two rival families. The musical, which dates from the 1950s (the film was released in 1961) inflects the action of the play towards contemporary 'social problems' (racial prejudice, street violence, youthful rebellion against authority) in a way that seems to confirm the story as of 'universal' significance. Yet in fact only one element of Shakespeare's structure has been employed, so that the story falls here into a quite different narrative and dramatic pattern.

Ultimately the question I am addressing resolves into a simple choice of alternative explanations. Does Shakespeare's *Romeo and Juliet* contain, within its narrative and dramatic structure, a story of universal application and consistent meaning, which can be mobilised to say virtually the same thing in many different cultural and historical situations? Or does the apparent 'timelessness' of the story derive from a continual reworking of the basic idea, to fit different cultural and historical situations, with each version being more a production of its own time and place than a restating of Shakespeare's text?

In the following pages we will be looking at variations between different versions and re-tellings of the 'Romeo and Juliet' story, both before and after Shakespeare's play; at differences between performances and printed texts and at some of the variety of different theatrical adaptations of the 'same' play in recent cultural history.

ﾟ৹

The obvious point to begin this exploration is with the play's own definition of its moral and ideological pattern. The action of the play is introduced by a 'Chorus', a figure of prescient wisdom like a narrator, who stands both inside and outside the action of the play and is, therefore, better able to deliver a judgement on the meaning of its dramatised events. The Chorus re-appears briefly at the beginning of Act II, but is not otherwise in evidence. Some producers have felt that it would be neater if the Chorus were there to sum up at the end of the play too: Franco Zeffirelli 's film version takes some lines from the Prince's concluding speech, and has them delivered in the voice-over commentary of the Chorus. The voice used, that of Lord Laurence Olivier, is a familiar theatrical voice, reverberant with cultural authority: so in this production the Chorus' interpretation of events is developed into a complete narrative frame, establishing a clear perspective from which we may judge and respond to the dramatic action.

At the play's opening the Chorus lays the basis for the story by outlining the feud between the two great houses, a quarrel rooted in inveterate enmity ('ancient grudge'), and now breaking out into reopened hostilities ('new mutiny'). We never learn what the quarrel was about in the first place. The significance of the relationship between Romeo and Juliet is placed by the Chorus firmly within the context of the feud: he calls them 'a pair of star-crossed lovers', lovers doomed to undergo a tragedy fated in their fortunes, written in their stars. The Chorus then makes it clear that this tragedy does however entail positive consequences, since the tragic deaths of Romeo and Juliet will bring their parents new understanding, will reconcile their deep-rooted familial enmity and pacify their habitual violence. The Chorus' speech stresses this aspect particularly strongly, repeating the claim by emphasising that nothing else but the deaths of their children could have healed the civil breach: he speaks of

> .... their parents' rage,
> Which, but their children's end, nought could remove ...
> (Prologue, 10-11)

The *Prologue* is in a sense a blue print for the action of the play, a model in miniature of its artistic and emotional structure. There is the feud, then there are the lovers whose passion transcends it; there is the paradoxical denouement in which the feuding families destroy the lovers, but are then redeemed by the example of their love. There is of course an element of contradiction in this structure: the love of Romeo and Juliet is the only good thing produced by the feud, yet it must be destroyed if the feud is to be reconciled. This element may seem disconcerting, even unpalatable; though the quality of contradiction involved in this 'sacrificial' interpretation of the play is regarded as appropriate to some conceptions of tragedy.

As we shall see, however, this contradictory structure, in which the death of the lovers is the price to be paid for a settling of the feud, represents a highly problematical aspect of *Romeo and Juliet*. Some dramatised versions of the play wholeheartedly embrace this interpretation: Franco Zeffirelli ended his screen version by adding to Shakespeare's text a double funeral procession, in which the bodies of Romeo and Juliet are borne through the streets of Verona and into the church. Members of the two families file on either side after the bodies and divide when they reach the camera, separated but joined by their mutual loss. The

heads of the families look across at one another, formally but
with obvious regret; the Nurse leans across and touches Benvolio,
then the servants who follow embrace or clasp hands. At the end
of *West Side Story*, members of both the rival street gangs help to
carry off the dead body of Tony (Romeo); and Maria (Juliet) sur-
vives, her bereavement a universal reproach.

On the other hand some of the play's adapters and producers
have clearly been very unhappy about some of the implications of
this 'sacrificial' view of *Romeo and Juliet*. One remarkable production, directed for the Royal Shakespeare Company by Michael
Bogdanov in 1986,[3] represents the deaths of the lovers as futile
and unnecessary, and casts a harshly ironic light on the reconciliation of the two families, who appear almost smug and compla-
cent as they unveil the golden statues of Romeo and Juliet,
emblems not so much of their children's sacrifice as of their own
wealth and generosity. Juliet's death was followed immediately by
a blackout: after a pause lights went up on the bodies of the
lovers, already converted into the statues promised by their
fathers at the end of the play-text. The Prince presided over the
unveiling of the statues, reading a cut version of the Chorus's *Prologue* from two note cards, while the two families gathered
around to pose for photographers. The spectacle of Capulet and
Montague shaking hands was performed as a public ceremony,
like two politicians at a summit conference. As most of the cast
left the stage, the emptiness and hypocrisy of the entire ritual
was thrown into perspective by some final additional details:
Lady Montague placed a flower at the foot of Romeo's statue,
and Benvolio left slowly and in dejection. Both these marginal
characters were distinguished, in their genuine sense of loss, from
the collective atmosphere of callous indifference and criminal
complacency.

The disagreement between these respective productions is
about what might be called the 'moral' of the story. They agree in
taking a positive view of the lovers themselves, and in regarding
their love as a healthy and therapeutic challenge to the casual

hostility and routine violence of a divided society. They agree in taking a negative view both of the feud and of the families who sustain it. Where they differ is over the question of whether the sacrificial deaths of the two lovers can be regarded as having a decisively beneficial effect on their society. Zeffirelli's film and *West Side Story* both show a newly awakened sense of remorse growing between the two factions, pointing towards peace and reconciliation. Bogdanov however proposes that the families which have callously exploited the innocence, youth and beauty of their children are merely continuing to do so, and if anything profiting from, rather than losing by, their deaths.

Although Bogdanov's production was criticised as a 'distortion' of the play, it clearly proposes a possible interpretation of the dramatic text. By the simple theatrical idea of using the lovers' own bodies, dressed in gold fabric, to represent the statues, Bogdanov stressed a conception already implicit in the Shakespearean text – that there is something meanly commercial and even competitive about the final speeches of Capulet and Montague, which seems out of keeping with the prevailing tragic emotion.

CAPULET
O brother Montague, give me thy hand.
This is my daughter's jointure, for no more
Can I demand.

MONTAGUE
              But I can give thee more.
For I will raise her statue in pure gold,
That whiles Verona by that name is known,
There shall no figure at such rate be set
As that of true and faithful Juliet.

CAPULET
As rich shall Romeo's by his lady lie,
Poor sacrifices of our enmity!
                              (V.3.296–302)

Of course these lines can be interpreted sympathetically, as indicative of a genuine change of heart in the leaders of both the families. We can infer that their strongest shared emotion is a sense of loss, and that they are very much aware of the poverty and bitterness of all that is left to them – two old men shaking hands, planning a memorial tribute to their slaughtered children; a poor substitute for the marriage alliance they might have mutually enjoyed.

At the same time, we might take a different view. The lovers are here envisaged as transformed from the shameful and piteous image of their stabbed and poisoned corpses, into decorative artistic objects, expressive of both aesthetic and material value. This combined emphasis on wealth and prettiness operates to conceal the brutal and uncomfortable truths the play has disclosed. Capulet admits that the lovers are '*poor* sacrifices': but both families are eager to change them back into something 'rich'. Both Montague and Capulet here speak a language of commercial transaction, sealing a parodic marriage contract in which the principals, being dead, are symbolically eliminated from their parents' financial preoccupations. If Montague does give Capulet his hand (the text does not indicate whether or not this is meant to occur) it may be more in the spirit of a bargain struck than a gesture of amity. Furthermore, the exchange is conducted as a kind of competition ('I can give thee more' ... 'as rich ... '), as if the two houses are still vying with one another for pre-eminence in wealth and status.

There seems to be no acknowledgement at all that Romeo and Juliet have been made victims of the families' competitive emulation (the feud, through which Romeo kills Tybalt) and of their hunger for status and power (the arranged marriage between Juliet and Paris), rather than of some abstract and inexplicable 'enmity'. In a play which continually sets love as a challenging value against the mercenary ethics of profit, competition and property marriage, there is surely something odd about the final reconciliation being formulated in precisely those terms; as if the two families are closing ranks very much in the old way, having expelled the unassimilable element of an inter-family relationship.

A similar basic structure can be open to quite different possibilities of interpretation. Other versions of the Romeo and Juliet story offer even more radically dissimilar interpretative perspectives. The primary source of Shakespeare's play was a long narrative poem. *The Tragicall History of Romeus and Juliet* (1562) by Arthur Brooke.[4] This was an English translation of a French version (by Francois Belleforest) of an Italian romance *Romeo e Giuiletta* (1554) by Matteo Bandello. At least two other versions of the story, one Italian (Luigi da Porto's *Giuletta e Romeo*, c. 1530), and another English translation (William Painter's 'Romeo and Julietta', included in *The Palace of Pleasure*, [vol II, 1567], are considered possible as source material: so the story was obviously a very popular one before Shakespeare adapted it for the stage. Brooke's translation is preceded by a Preface (*To the Reader*) in which the translator offers his evaluation of the story's meaning. It is an account very different from that given by the Chorus in Shakespeare's play.

> The good man's example biddeth men to be good, and the evil man's mischief warneth men not to be evil … And to this end (good Reader) is this tragicall matter written, to describe unto thee a couple of unfortunate lovers, thralling themselves to unhonest desire, neglecting the authority and advice of parents and friends, conferring their principal counsels with drunken gossips, and superstitious friars (the naturally fit instruments of unchastity) attempting all adventures of peril, for the attaining of their wished lust, using auricular confession (the key of whoredom, and treason) for furtherance of their purpose, abusing the honourable name of lawful marriage, to cloak unhappy death.

Here the story is offered as exemplifying a clear and uncompromising moral lesson. The reader should consider the fates of these two lovers, obsessed by illicit passion, rebelling against the legitimate authority of family, church and state, trusting in immoral and superstitious assistants (the Nurse and the Friar), abusing the sacrament of marriage; and their example should clearly point the way towards the desirability of an honest and temperate life, embracing virtue and shunning vice. This is not of course the way Shakespeare's play is normally read or produced. Yet Brooke's poem is not only a version of the same story, it is Shakespeare's principal source. Is Brooke's Preface a possible interpretation of the story? Critics have dealt with this difficulty in various ways: by arguing that Brooke's poem offers a perspective different from his own Preface; that the puritanical translator was just using the Preface for an opportunistic dig at the Catholics; or that Brooke's poem does indeed construct of the story a simple moral fable, while Shakespeare's play is an infinitely more complex and ambiguous poetic drama. But none of these arguments quite confronts the sharp divergences between this *negative* view of the lovers as culpable moral delinquents who bring about their own downfall, and the more familiar *positive* view of Romeo and Juliet as passionate dissenters within a corrupt and condemned society. Yet some critical interpretations of the play, notably that of W.H. Auden, have indeed taken this line, and interpreted the lovers as moral exempla of excessive passion.[5]

Not only do different versions of the same story offer different possibilities of interpretation: the *same* version of the story – e.g. Shakespeare's play – is by itself susceptible to varying emphases, differential readings, divergent interpretations. There are two ways of approaching this problem critically: one is to argue for the superiority of one particular interpretation over another, seeking to demonstrate and prove that a particular critical line fits the play best, or is more in keeping with its historical context, or is more appropriate to its written or theatrical form. The other is to assume that these various different readings, being possible interpretations of the text, are in some way contained in it, or at least potentially implied by it. If we can trace those readings to their origins in the text, we may arrive at a more complex and comprehensive account of the text's poetic and theatrical possibilities.

I would like to draw together some of these threads of inquiry into an extended discussion of one particular section of the play: that in which Juliet is commanded by her parents to marry Paris (III.5). This could be described as a point at which the play's 'universality' is very much apparent and to the fore. The key dramatic confrontation is between Juliet, cherishing and concealing her secret marriage to Romeo, and her parents, who have decided to over ride her inclinations and to force the arranged marriage to Paris. Romeo has been banished for causing the death of Tybalt. As spectators we of course are in full possession of the whole situation, so we naturally feel for Juliet's predicament. The conflict draws the two generations into a recognisable and familiar confrontation: the young, innocent in their simple need to love, helpless victims of family violence and family authority; the old, ignorant and insensitive, motivated by considerations of family wealth, status and power, forcing their child into a loveless union with a conventionally acceptable suitor. Calculated to speak with equal eloquence to the passions of the young and the consciences of the old, this scene seems to exemplify perfectly the play's capacity to appeal to a continually changing historical world which yet retains in place certain fundamental human problems.

How much scope does there seem to be here for diversity of interpretation? Would it be possible, for example, to apply the moralistic critique of Romeo and Juliet as passionate rebels against social order, religious sanctions and legitimate authority? Can we read the scene from the point of view of the older generation, responding with critical disapproval to the lovers, and with sympathetic admiration for the anxious solicitude of the parents? Or are we obliged rather to view the scene from only one possible perspective, responding to it as an affirmation of love, an uninhibited celebration of the uncompromising idealism of that supreme passion?

I would like to examine this scene in two separate forms: as it appears in the Zeffirelli film and as it appears in the Shakespeare text. Zeffirelli's film treatment is in general an attempt at making the play accessible to a modern audience, and in particular a youthful audience. The casting of two very young and relatively unknown actors (Olivia Hussey and Leonard Whiting) as the principal characters, and the radical cutting of the Elizabethan text to produce an easily intelligible screenplay, both testify to Zeffirelli's determination to make the play speak directly to young contemporary cinema-goers, rather than to the established audience of the theatres. Here then we have an example of a production-text based on a conception of the play as perpetually reproducible and consistently contemporary.

Naturally then in the film this scene is interpreted as an uncompromising endorsement of the lovers and an unmistakable critique of the parents. The opening sequence of the scene, which shows the lovers waking and parting, is filmed with great visual beauty and deep emotional intensity, heavily underlined by the romantic musical score. The sequence consists of close-ups of the naked lovers in bed, intercut with shots taken across the bed and towards the window of Juliet's bedroom. The scene is therefore suffused with a delicate dawn light, and our attention is pointed outwards from the interior of the room towards the beauty of the world outside. Another sequence then follows, in which Juliet leads Romeo along the balcony outside her window – the scene of their original vows of love. Romeo descends into the garden and leaves with a brief 'adieu'. A functional 'narrative' shot then shows Romeo mounting his horse and leaving the gates of Verona.

For the next sequence we are back in Juliet's bedroom but now the camera is angled inwards, towards the opposite wall: we are now confined in a domestic interior with no romantic other-world in view. Juliet's mother and the Nurse stand beside the bed, where Juliet sobs for Romeo. As in most of this film script, the text is cut substantially. From lines 60-103 of III.5 the film retains only the following lines of dialogue:

LADY CAPULET
We will have vengeance for it, fear thou not.
Then weep no more. I'll send to one in Mantua,
Where that same banished runagate doth live,
Shall give him such an unaccustomed dram
That he shall soon keep Tybalt company.
                                        (III.5.87-91)

Juliet says nothing, and simply continues to weep. The play-text at this point is continually associating love and death in a series of images, allusions and dramatic ironies. Obviously the plot itself is linking them firmly together, since we know that the death of Tybalt is the direct cause of Romeo's banishment. But the text goes much further than this, developing imagery which points towards the final re-uniting of Tybalt, Juliet and Romeo in the Capulet tomb. Although the film has cut most of the dialogue that contains this synthesis, it has its own visual imagery of death which displays in its own way no less beauty and power. Juliet's bed is surrounded by transparent, white gauze curtains. Lady Capulet begins her lines, which speak of the death of Tybalt and the projected murder of Romeo, from behind the curtains. The same white fabric will cover the supposedly 'dead' Juliet when she is carried to her first, mock funeral. In the Capulet tomb all the family corpses, including that of Tybalt, will be covered with the same transparent shroud. When in the final scene Romeo enters the tomb, he draws the shroud from the sleeping Juliet to kiss her 'corpse', before administering to himself an 'unaccustomed dram'. Through the subtle and entirely naturalistic repetition of a visual image, Zeffirelli links the bed of love with the couch of death, the violence of the feud with the violence of the lovers' suicide, the poison of revenge with self-destruction by poisoning.

The crucial difference in this respect between film-text and play-text is that this imagery of love-in-death and death-in-love is predominantly visual and is barely verbalised at all. Even where it is given verbal form, its impact is often lost through the choice of setting. Lady Capulet's line 'I would the fool were married to her grave' (III.5.140) is in the film spoken to Capulet in a corridor of the house rather than in Juliet's bedroom. The physical imagery of wedding bed/grave is not at that point visually there to complement the verbal association. The artistic impression given by this visualisation of metaphor is that the contradictory or ironic linking of love and violence, passion and death, is *circumstantial* rather than any part of the lovers' own experience. They remain innocent, untouched by the contamination of violence, victims of rather than participants in the pervasive imagery of love-in-death, death-in-love.

In the play-text it is quite a different matter. Juliet herself speaks a poetic language saturated with these contradictory associations. As Romeo leaves, she defines separation as a kind of death, and instinctively though unwittingly predicts the eventual outcome of their relationship:

> JULIET
> Methinks I see the, now thou art so slow,
> As one dead in the bottom of a tomb.
> (III.5.55-6)

In the sequence between Juliet and her mother, there is a strong verbal emphasis on the paradoxical quality of her grief, which is actually directed towards Romeo, but seems to be occasioned by the death of Tybalt. Juliet speaks throughout in full awareness of this double perspective, constructing a complex verbal play around the related ideas of death, murder, revenge, love, separation and sex. 'No man doth grieve my heart' like Romeo, Juliet claims, professing a sorrow for Tybalt and a hatred of his murderer.

> LADY CAPULET
> That is because the traitor murderer lives.
>
> JULIET
> Ay madam, from the reach of these my hands.
> Would none but I might venge my cousin's death! ...
> ... O, how my heart abhors

> To hear him named and cannot come to him,
> To wreak the love I bore my cousin
> Upon his body that hath slaughtered him!
>
> (III.5.84-6, 99-102)

Juliet's wordless sobbing in the film contrasts sharply with this sophisticated verbalisation of a contradictory synthesis of love and violence, passion and death. The juxtaposition, in the last line, of the idea of a violent assault with the idea of a passionate embrace, seems to suggest that Juliet's emotions are deeply coloured by the circumstances in which they have to be negotiated.

By the time Capulet enters to harangue his daughter with a crude and violent language of paternalistic authoritarianism, each of these two performance-texts has constructed a different perspective on the experience of the lovers themselves. There can be, on the other hand, only one view of Capulet's behaviour. Everything in the text points towards a critical response to his patriarchal bullying: his original scruples about Juliet's own opinion, now abandoned; his callous dismissal of Tybalt's death ('Well, we were born to die', III.4.4); his obvious determination not to let the inconvenience of bereavement cause an eligible suitor to slip out of his net.

In this respect the play seems to be operating quite simply to validate the lovers and to condemn the father. But the play-text itself, on the other hand, unlike the film, does not quite affirm the lovers as innocent and uncontaminated. Theirs is after all a love born of violence and hatred: while Zeffirelli's text suggests that passion can transcend the circumstances of its genesis, the play-text indicates that a love engendered from conflict is likely to harbour dangerous tendencies, to conceal beneath its glamorous surface impulses of violent self-destruction, a passion for annihilation, a deep lust for death.

It should be possible to look again at that 'older generation' of the Capulet family, and consider whether or not we as spectators are obliged to view them from Juliet's point of view – as a solid conspiracy of callous and insensitive authoritarians, trying to impose their corrupt and mercenary values on the passion and innocence of youth. As we have seen, Capulet is a fairly straight-forward case: there seems little room for debate about how we should judge him. But what of Juliet's mother? Is she not trying to do the best for her daughter on the basis of her own values? Does she not also intercede for Juliet against her father's rage? And what of the Nurse? Her recommendation to Juliet – that she should make the best of a bad job, forget Romeo and marry Paris – however crude and utilitarian it may be, is obviously offered with the best of intentions and out of a conviction that there is no escape from the tightly wound knot of circumstances in which they are all trapped. These three parental figures actually represent different points of view, and coalesce into a solid conspiracy only in Juliet's imagination.

The truth of the matter is that Juliet's love no longer has (if it ever had) any social space to occupy. There simply is no means (if there ever was) to integrate the relationship of Romeo and Juliet into the existing social structure. Juliet is bound in a clan destine marriage to the son of her father's enemy, who is now also the murderer of her cousin. If she remains committed to that relationship, she remains estranged from all the structures that give shape to her society. A love so alienated from any possibility of social integration turns quite naturally to desperate passion, to violent self-destruction, to the hopeless remedy of suicide. And that is Juliet's ultimate acknowledgement, delivered at the end of this scene: 'If all else fail, myself have power to die' (III.5.243). An idealistic passion utterly estranged from its society can in the last resort claim only one remedy, boast only one power: the capacity for self-annihilation. 'These violent delights' as Friar Laurence warned, 'have violent ends' (II.6.9).

I am not suggesting that this type of reading can return us to a simple moralistic interpretation of the play: we are not left here with an Awful Warning against the perils of unbridled passion. But we have, in recognising these aspects of the play, complicated that initial idea of *Romeo and Juliet* as a simple celebration of pure love pitted against the corrupt powers of social division and mercenary morality. Perhaps moralistic readers like Arthur Brooke and W.H. Auden were responding to something in the play-text: something which does not perhaps point towards a moralistic reading quite in the way they proposed, but does at least make a romantic and 'circumstantial' interpretation like Zeffirelli's, in which love is portrayed as pure and positive, problematical and hard to sustain.

Clearly then, it is possible to find sharp divergences of interpretation in these dramatised forms of the play – between Zeffirelli's conclusion, and Bogdanov's; or between Zeffirelli's interpretation of the lovers, and others we can find in the play-text itself. Every performance, every production of *Romeo and Juliet* is an act of interpretation, more or less liberal in its approach to the text. Some producers feel obliged to accept the received form of the text (i.e. the agreed scholarly consensus recorded in a modern edition) as the basis for their dramatic interpretations: for example the BBC/Time-Life Shakespeare series operated a policy of using 'complete', relatively uncut texts. Other producers adopt a much freer, more original approach, using the text largely as a basis for their independent creative activity. Such adaptations are often criticised for their failure to respect the original. But it can be argued that free adaptations of Elizabethan drama, where the production ends up with a version which is quite different from the printed play-text, is more in keeping with the historical character of Renaissance drama than a production which dutifully follows the received text.

Let us attempt to locate the play-text into the physical space of the Elizabethan theatre. Consider first the question of *location*. Where do events usually happen in this play? The Elizabethan theatres used a bare stage without scenery: so there was no representation of *place* as there often is in modern theatres, or in film or television adaptations. At the beginning of I.2, we would naturally assume that Capulet and Paris are conversing in the former's house. The servant does not actually go anywhere: Capulet and Paris go out leaving him alone on stage. When Benvolio and Romeo appear and meet him, it becomes obvious that this certainly cannot be Capulet's house. When, in the eighteenth century, scholars began to edit Elizabethan play-texts, editors would often supply a location: Edward Capell, for example, publishing an edition of the plays in 1768,[6] got around this difficulty by prescribing 'Verona, a street' as the location of the whole scene, and many subsequent editions followed suit. This provides a natural enough place in which Romeo and Benvolio can meet the Clown but it seems correspondingly awkward to assume that Capulet should discuss his daughter's marriage with a distinguished suitor in the street too!

In all Elizabethan theatres, this did not really present a problem at all. Since the stage did not represent any particular place, it could be imagined as representing any place necessary or convenient for the scene. An Elizabethan audience would have been quite happy to think of the earlier part of the scene taking place in Capulet's house, and then to assume that the location had changed to a street before the Clown meets Romeo and Benvolio. Simply by walking across the stage, the Clown could suggest a change of location, without the visible appearance of the stage changing at all.

Later in Act I, Scene 4, Romeo, Mercutio and their companions talk about gate-crashing Capulet's feast. They are carrying torches, partly to indicate that the scene is set at night. At the end of their conversation, they do not leave the stage to undertake that journey but instead they perform a pantomimic trip around the stage to the Capulet house. The Elizabethan texts[7] show that the Montagues did not actually go off but remained on stage: '*They march about the stage*'. The Capulet servants simultaneously bring on the properties of the feast: '*They march about the stage; and Servingmen come forth with napkins*'. When the Capulets enter, the stage direction makes it clear that the disguised Montagues stay where they are and the Capulets come forward to greet them: '*Enter Capulet, his wife, Juliet, Tybalt, Nurse, and all the guests and gentlemen to the maskers*'. The Montagues stay where they are, the Capulet servants bring in the feast, the family and other guests arrive by entering the stage area – the Montagues do not go to the feast, the feast comes to them. In an Elizabethan performance, in other words, the revellers would simply walk around the stage to indicate that they were 'going somewheres' – i.e. walking to, and entering, Capulet's house. Again, eighteenth century editors would substitute for the original stage directions an *Exeunt*, clearing the stage so that the Capulet feast could be staged by a re-setting of the scene, moving the location into Capulet's house. More modern editions, like the New Penguin Shakespeare text, go back to the original texts, use their stage directions, and prescribe no fixed location for individual scenes.

We are today accustomed to dramatic media such as television and film, which represent location directly and unmistakably, by filming their physical equivalents – a city, a domestic interior, a forest, a sea-shore. The editors of the eighteenth and nineteenth centuries, who laid the basis for our modern Shakespeare texts, were accustomed to a theatre in which location was established by the use of pictorial scenery, and maintained by frequent and elaborate scene-changes. Hence eighteenth and nineteenth century texts prescribe different location, and imply theatrical scene-changes, within their construction of the dramatic narrative.

Let us look for example at the last 'movement' of the play, which begins with Juliet taking the poison (in IV.3). In an Elizabethan theatre in or around the 1590s, the stage would not have changed its appearance at all throughout the sequence of events. That of course was standard practice and nothing unusual. What makes this sequence particularly remarkable is the fact that Juliet's drugged and unconscious body was obviously intended to *remain on stage* throughout the rest of the play. The location of the performance alters to somewhere else in the Capulet house

(IV.4), back to Juliet's bedroom (IV.5), to Romeo in Mantua (V.1), to Friar Laurence's cell (V.2), to the Capulet monument (V.3). But in Elizabethan stagings, Juliet clearly remained on stage: at the end of IV.3, where the 'Second Quarto' text gives no stage direction, and the Folio gives *Exit* (a direction which would, if followed, commit the actress to a clumsy stagger off stage), the 'First Quarto' states precisely: '*She falls upon her bed, within the curtains*'.

Precisely *where* on the stage she would have rested requires further discussion and comment. Much scholarly discussion of the staging of Elizabethan plays has worked on the assumption that the theatres had, in addition to the resources detailed above, an inner stage or 'discovery space' at the back of the platform stage, recessed into the 'tiring-house', which could have been closed off from the above sequence of scenes in a manner relatively easy to organise: Juliet would actually disappear from view of the audience by falling through the curtains onto a 'bed' inside the recessed inner stage. Subsequent scenes like IV.4 could then have been played with those curtains closed, and Juliet completely hidden. The Nurse would have 'discovered' her sleeping (apparently dead) form by drawing back the curtains. Closing them again would leave the stage clear for V.1 and V.2, and in V.3 they could be drawn again to symbolise the opening of the Capulet tomb.

My view is that there was no such 'inner stage', at least in the theatre where and when *Romeo and Juliet* was originally performed. Without an inner stage, Juliet's bed would have had to be, and to remain, on the main stage, and scenes like IV.4, V.1 and V.2 played under the conventional pretence that the characters on stage would be unaware of the heroine lying there, unconscious and partly concealed. The 'curtains' would be curtains around the bed, not stage curtains fencing off a separate acting area. That pattern of staging would require a non-naturalistic method of performance in which the bed and its occupant could be excluded from, or brought into view, according to the requirements of the dramatic narrative. Even if there was an inner stage, this scene could still not have worked naturalistically: since the same physical object would have had to change its significance from one scene to another, beginning as a piece of furniture in a girl's bedroom, and ending as a bier in her family vault. So the physical resources of the stage clearly worked in a symbolic, emblematic way rather than, like the stage technology of later theatres, aiming at a convincing 'realism' of dramatic presentation.

In the New Penguin Shakespeare text of *Romeo and Juliet*, the action is divided into scenes as follows:

IV.3   Juliet drinks the potion.

IV.4   Capulets prepare for the wedding.

IV.5   Nurse discovers Juliet 'dead'.

V.1   Balthasar tells Romeo of Juliet's 'death'. Romeo buys poison from the Apothecary.

V.2   Friar Laurence meets Friar John, learns of the disastrous miscarriage of the message.

V.3   Paris enters the churchyard; Romeo appears and breaks open the tomb, kills Paris, commits suicide. Juliet wakes, finds Romeo dead, kills herself. The Prince and the two families arrive to find them dead.

Although this text does not fix the scenes in particular locations, it still divides some sequences into separate scenes, even though in fact the normal principle of scene-division – that the stage is cleared and other characters enter – does not apply. Most of the original texts – including the 'Second Quarto' and the 'Folio' – have no scene divisions at all. The First Quarto indicates a break between sections of narrative, at the points where later editors made scene-divisions, by inserting a row of printer's ornaments between the passages of text. This device would have told the actors where a change of stage personnel occurred: but it did not of course carry the same implications as a modern 'change of scene'. Eighteenth century editors formalised those breaks into scene-divisions to accommodate the play to their own type of theatre, where scene-shifts would actually be made by the

changing of pictorial scenery. Thus in eighteenth century editions of the play, and in later editions which followed them, you
would find these now separate scenes set in different locations.[8]

 IV.3 *Juliet's Chamber*
 IV.4 *A Hall*
 IV.5 *SCENE changes to Juliet's chamber,* Juliet *on a bed.*
 V.1   *Mantua. A street.*
 V.2   *Verona. Friar Laurence's cell.*
 V.3   *Verona; a churchyard; in it a tomb belonging to the Capulets*

None of this could have applied to the Elizabethan stage, where
locations could not have been fixed in this way. They only make
sense for a theatre where movable scenery supplies location by
the visual representation of a particular place. The introductory
stage direction for IV.4 actually states that the '*SCENE changes*': in
an eighteenth century theatre this would have involved a painted
backcloth being drawn aside to reveal another one.[9] Another
eighteenth century edition[10] has a different direction for this passage: *Ante-room of Juliet's chamber. Door of the Chamber open,
and* Juliet *upon her bed.* To stage this conception a theatre would
have to be able to construct the appearance of two separate
rooms on the stage.

In an eighteenth century theatre the final scene would have
been similarly elaborate: when David Garrick produced *Romeo
and Juliet* in the mid-eighteenth century, the stage had a large set-
construction representing the tomb, with tall double doors, erect-
ed in front of a backcloth painted to resemble the churchyard – a
night sky, trees, moonlight.[11] The first part of the scene took place
before the closed tomb; Romeo broke open the doors and entered
the tomb to join Juliet. In later theatres this elaborate staging was
extended even further: in a nineteenth century theatre the initial
action in the churchyard, and the subsequent action in the tomb,
were performed on separate sets, with the curtain drawn to cover
the scene-change.[12] When Henry Irving played Romeo at the
Lyceum theatre in the 1880s, these two parts of the scene occupied
completely different locations: the action before the tomb was

played on a churchyard-set, which was removed behind the curtain; and the action within the tomb performed on another large stage set, complete with stone walls, vaulted arches, and at the rear of the stage a staircase leading upwards, flooded with moonlight from the churchyard where the previous scene had taken place.[13] Clearly such devices of staging belong to a theatre very different from the bare, unfurnished open space of the Elizabethan stage: but by the time we get to Irving's production, the stage is obviously trying to emulate the theatrical realism later made possible by the medium of film.

Let us consider how differently this 'movement' of the play is constructed in Zeffirelli's modern film version. Film narrative normally operates naturalistically, either by shooting actual locations, or faking them by means of a studio set. *Romeo and Juliet* was filmed over a large number of different locations in Italy, since the director wanted to fill his screen with vivid naturalistic images of Renaissance society and culture. Here is a summary of the film's treatment of these final scenes, taken from Jack Jorgen's *Shakespeare on Film*.[14] The initial number represents a division of the film-text into separate 'scenes', each of which occupies a particular location or studio setting; the number of the filmic 'scene' is followed by the Act and scene division of Shakespeare's text. Most of the filmic 'scenes' have no corresponding Act and scene division, since they have no exact counterpart in Shakespeare's text.

22. (4.3) Juliet's room. Juliet pulls shut the white gauze bedcurtain, drinks the potion.

23. Outside Friar Laurence's cell. Morning. Friar Laurence sends a Brother on a donkey with the letter to Romeo.

24. (4.5) Capulet's house. Birds sing. Nurse's cry pierces the quiet: 'Juliet is dead!' The Capulets rush to find it is so.

25. The Road to Mantua. The Brother proceeds slowly.

26.(4.5) Capulet's tomb. Romeo's man watches Juliet's funeral, rides down tree-lined road.

27. Road to Mantua. Romeo's man races past the brother.

28.   Mantua. Romeo's man arrives, tells him Juliet is dead.
29.   Road to Verona. Romeo rides past Brother, through sheep.
30. (5.3) Verona Churchyard. Night. Romeo dismisses his man,
         breaks open the doors of the crypt, passes by rows of rotting
         corpses to find Juliet. He takes off her shroud, kisses her.
         Seeing Tybalt's body, he walks to it and asks her forgiveness.
         He holds Juliet once again, weeps, drinks poison. The Friar
         arrives too late. As Juliet wakes he hears the Prince's
         trumpet, urges her to flee, goes out. She finds Romeo, kisses
         him, weeps, stabs herself.
31.(5.3) Verona Square. Two families united in a funeral procession.
         Prince angrily: 'All are punished!' Chorus: 'A glooming peace
         this morning with it brings./ The sun for sorrow will not
         show his head./For never was a story of more woe/Than this
         of Juliet and her Romeo'. Members of the two families make
         gestures of reconciliation, pass by leaving shot of castellated
         tower and walls of Verona.

The most obvious area of innovation in the film treatment is the
addition of scenes depicting pieces of action which in the play-
text are narrated or only implied. The plot at this point obviously
involves an action spread over space and time, with people moving between one place and another. In a *narrative* medium, all
this circumstantial detail would of course be related: Shakespeare's primary source, Brooke's *The Tragical History of Romeus
and Juliet* (1562), spends almost 1,000 lines describing these concluding events. But in the *dramatic* text all this narrative detail is
severely condensed: we have the Friar's indication that he has a
plan, at the end of IV.1, and the arrival of Balthasar in Mantua at
the beginning of V.1. Apart from these details, the only scene with
a purely narrative function that the play seems to have needed
is the brief exchange between Friar Laurence and Friar John in
V.2. The film however supplies a running description of the
whole plot, by adding six scenes on the road between Verona and
Mantua.

It could obviously be argued that the condensed nature of the dramatic text was more a matter of limitation than strength: since the stage could not *show* time or place, dramatists simply had to work around the constraints of their medium. The development of film technology enabled the dramatic art to occupy those dimensions of space and time that were always at the disposal of the narrative forms such as the epic, the romance and the novel. If Shakespeare had been able, as Zeffirelli was, to deploy a dramatic technology capable of representing the delays and over-hasty dashes that precipitate the tragedy, he would surely, we may feel, have welcomed it. But it is worth remembering that *Romeo and Juliet* was written for the theatre of its time, and worth considering what dramatic potentialities that relationship between dramatist and medium entailed.

Let us return to Juliet's simulated suicide (IV.3), and relocate the action of the play into the performance space of the Elizabethan public theatre. Juliet withdraws and takes her potion in the midst of the busy bustle and preparation of the Capulet household. IV.2 and IV.4 are simply one continuous action, with Capulet, his lady and the Nurse making their preparations for the wedding feast. As we have seen, when Juliet takes the drug, the stage directions indicate that from this point on in Elizabethan performance, the rest of the play would have been performed continuously, with Juliet never leaving the stage. On drinking the potion '*She falls upon her bed within the curtains*'. Her mother and Nurse enter the stage, though they are not supposed to be in Juliet's bedroom. Capulet and several servants also pass across the stage, while Juliet in her bed remains in full view of the audience. It is only when the Nurse is told to wake her that she moves to the stage-bed, discovers Juliet apparently dead, and calls the attention of the other characters to the girl's silence presence.

The poetic language of the play persistently draws analogies with the maiden's own bed, the wedding bed she should have occupied and the tomb she occupies in her simulated death. On the Elizabethan stage these were not merely metaphors, since the dramatic action demanded that they be one and the same physical location. When the Friar and Paris enter, they insistently link, in a series of choric laments, love and death, sexual union and dying, the marriage bed and the grave. The obvious parallel between analogous rituals, wedding and funeral, evokes a terrible similarity in the midst of grotesque contrast.

When the characters leave, the stage direction indicates that the Nurse closes the curtain round her bed which is obviously all the burial Juliet would get on the Elizabethan stage. The tragic atmosphere is then subverted by a comic scene with the atmosphere of mourning and bereavement. But then of course (and this is perhaps the point of the interlude) since Juliet is not truly dead, and will soon be reunited with her husband Romeo, the humorous jesting of a wedding feast is perhaps more appropriate to the truth of the situation – i.e. that if all goes according to plan the lovers will shortly be free and reunited – than the sadness of a funeral

Further analogies between the bed and the grave then appear at the beginning of V.1, as Romeo awaits news of Juliet. He has dreamed that Juliet found him dead, and revived him with a kiss. The vividness of the dream, and its mythical basis in fairy tale (though normally it is the sleeping maiden who is resurrected by the kiss of a man) convince him that it is an augury of truth. The speech is replete with dramatic ironies: in the event it is Juliet who will wake from apparent death, and her kissing of the dead Romeo, designed to drink up any remaining poison, will be part of her determination to join him in death.

The Elizabethan stage thrived on this dramatic interplay of contradictions: comedy and tragedy, mirth and funeral, love and death, always had to occupy the same physical space, and to co-exist in a brief and eventual space of time, 'the two-hours traffic of our stage'. Those developments in theatrical and film technologies which enabled producers to *separate* the different elements, placing them further apart by scene-changes or film editing, may have added a dimension of realism, but may also have detracted from the union of physical and verbal power this particular dramatic text possessed in its original theatrical context of performance.

Certainly the Zeffirelli film, building on the pictorial stage realism practised in the eighteenth century theatre and recorded in the eighteenth century editions of Shakespeare, was thus able to produce a performance interpretation of the play quite different from anything that could have been produced on the Elizabethan stage. While the former clearly presents an accessible modern Shakespeare, it also simplifies the possibilities of meaning latent in the theatrical text, delivering a more purely romantic *Romeo and Juliet* than the Elizabethan playgoer witnessed around 1595.

In this observation mere nostalgia for a theatre long since vanished beneath the rubble of time (and very quickly, whenever traces of it surface, buried again by the property developers)? Perhaps so: but the complex capacity for a pluralistic performance still rests within the dramatic text, and can still be released by the right combination of historical insight and modern theatrical ingenuity. Think for example of a famous scene from *West Side Story* (not the balcony-scene, but the equivalent of Romeo and Juliet, III.2), in which Tony and Maria, independently anticipating that night's meeting, sing (separately but in unison) 'Tonight, tonight, won't be just any night … ', while the two rival street gangs, again separated in space but united in music, contribute an aggressive disharmony in their version of the same number: 'We're gonna have a rumble, tonight … '. Here the musical score in which each separate element has a place provides an artistic space similar to the unified world of the Elizabethan platform stage. The film technique of 'intercutting' enables the four separate parties (Tony, Maria, the Jets and the Sharks) to be juxtaposed on screen, not simultaneously but in rapid sequence, although each is to be imagined as occupying an unrelated physical space. The musical score links these separate elements in a complex but indissoluble unity, an interplay of harmony and discord, precisely parallel to the complex unity of the Elizabethan public stage. This is just one example of a performance-text which brings us close to the true dramatic and theatrical nature of Romeo and Juliet.

Notes

ॐ

Preface

1 Anthony Davies, 'Shakespeare and the Media of Film, Radio and Television', *Shakespeare Survey*, 39 (1987), p. 1.

2 This canon is discussed in Chapter Four.

3 Robert Shaughnessy, ed., *Shakespeare on Film* (London: Macmillan, 1998), pp. 2–3.

4 Robert Lapsley and Michael Westlake, *Film Theory: an Introduction* (Manchester, 1988), p. vii.

5 Commenting on that 1985 essay, Anthony Davies suggested that 'The extent to which film and television do have the potential to re-establish Shakespeare as a popular dramatist and the degree to which various cultural authorities will continue to attempt the imposition of traditional Shakespeare orthodoxy is … certainly one of the most challenging issues to arise from the media's adoption of Shakespeare and it will assuredly continue to provoke dynamic debate. For when Holderness proposes that "the most promising space for cultural intervention remains, despite systematic attacks on the system, that of education" he is locating the debate where it ought to be', (Davies, 'Shakespeare and the Media', p. 11).

6 See John Collick, *Shakespeare, Cinema and Society* (Manchester: Manchester University Press, 1989): 'Radical developments in literary and cultural analysis over the last ten years have now provided us with a means of breaking out of the closed loop of formalist and prescriptive Shakespeare analysis, and a way of contextualising both

it and the films themselves in their social and historical moments. Writers such as Catherine Belsey, Graham Holderness, Noel Burch and Michael Chanan have already begun to do this. The strategies that have been adopted seek to identify the cultural and historical source of a text or a film's meaning. Instead of suggesting that the meaning of a text is the product of a single artistic consciousness this approach recognises that its form, content and cultural position is determined by the economic and political forces that condition its production' (p. 8).

One: Bard on the Box (1985, 1988)

The first part of this chapter was originally published as 'Boxing the Bard: Shakespeare and Television', in *The Shakespeare Myth*, edited by Graham Holderness (Manchester: Manchester University Press, 1988), pp. 173–189. The second part as 'Radical Potentiality and Institutional Closure: Shakespeare in Film and Television', edited by Jonathan Dollimore and Alan Sinfield (Manchester: MUP, 1985), pp. 182–201.

1   1574 patent granted by Elizabeth I to 'Leicester's Men'. See E.K. Chambers, *The Elizabethan Stage* (Oxford: Clarendon Press, 1923), II, pp. 87–8.

2   Royal Charter granted to the British Broadcasting Corporation, 1981.

3   See Graham Holderness, *Shakespeare's History* (Dublin: Gill and Macmillan, 1985), pp. 153–60.

4   William Maley, 'Centralisation and censorship', in Colin MacCabe and Olivia Stewart (eds), *The BBC and Public Service Broadcasting* (Manchester: Manchester University Press, 1986), pp. 35–6.

5   The evidence of Mr J.C.W. Reith to the Crawford Committee, December 1925 – see R.A. Coase, *British Broadcasting: a Study in Monopoly* (London: Longman, 1950); J.C.W. Reith, *Broadcasting over Britain* (London: Hodder, 1924), p. 196.

6   John Reith, quoted in MaCabe and Stewart, *The BBC*, p. 46.

7   Krishan Kumar, 'Public service broadcasting and the public interest', in MacCabe and Stewart, *The BBC*, p. 50.

8   George More O'Ferrall, 'The televising of drama', *Radio Times* (19 March 1937), p. 4.

9   John Wilders, 'Adjusting the set', *Times Literary Supplement* (10 July 1981), p. 13.

10 Raymond Williams, *Television: Technology and Cultural Form* (London: Fontana, 1974), pp. 88–90.

11 See John Drakakis, 'The essence that's not seen', in Peter Lewis, (ed.) *Radio Drama* (London: Longman, 1981). Janet Clare's list of radio productions in *Theatre of the Air: a checklist of radio productions of Renaissance drama, 1922–1986; Renaissance Drama Newsletter, Supplement Six* (University of Warwick, 1986) reveals that BBC radio had broadcast some one hundred productions of non-Shakespearean Renaissance plays, to over two hundred productions of Shakespeare; BBC television had broadcast just over one hundred Shakespeare productions, and *sixteen* non-Shakespearean plays. Stuart Evans discusses the technical problems of dramatising Shakespeare for radio in *Shakespeare Survey*, 39 (1986).

12 Philip Brockbank informed me that he recalled listening to this broadcast. The nightingale, unpatriotically insensible to the occasion, failed to show up.

13 After the war studio production became the norm, but there were several outside broadcasts from the Open Air Theatre, Regent's Park. *As You Like It* was adapted for studio, and *A Midsummer Night's Dream* broadcast from Regent's Park, in July 1946. See Ian Atkins, 'Open air theatre to studio', *Radio Times* (12 July 1946). See also Graham Holderness and Christopher J. McCullough, 'Shakespeare on the screen: a selective filmography', *Shakespeare Survey*, 39 (1986), p. 16 and p. 28.

14 *Hamlet*, produced by George More O'Ferrall, broadcast between 5 and 15 December 1947.

15 See J.C. Trewin, 'Every inch a king', *Radio Times* (20 August 1948), and 'A tragedy of darkness', *Radio Times* (18 February 1949), p. 25; and Lionel Hale, 'Othello – a play bursting with energy', *Radio Times* (21 April 1950), p. 43.

16 Panel discussion on 'Shakespeare and television', broadcast 22 April 1952.

17 *Radio Times* (15 May 1953); see p. 15 for feature article 'New Elizabethan actors'.

18 Terence Hawkes, *Shakespeare's Talking Animals* (London: Edward Arnold, 1973), p. 231.

19 John Wilders, 'Adjusting the set', *Times Higher Education Supplement* (10 July 1981), p. 13.

20 'Cedric Messina discusses *The Shakespeare Plays*', *Shakespeare Quarterly*, 30 (1979), p. 137.

21 Cedric Messina, 'Preface' to *The BBC TV Shakespeare: Richard II* (London: BBC, 1978), p. 8.

22 Ann Pasternak Slater, 'An interview with Jonathan Miller', *Quarto*, 10 (1980), p. 9.

23 Tim Hallinan, 'Jonathan Miller on *The Shakespeare Plays*', *Shakespeare Quarterly*, 32 (1981), p. 134.

24 Paul Johnson, '*Richard II*', in Roger Sales (ed.), *Shakespeare in Perspective* (London: BBC/Ariel Books, 1982), p. 33.

25 Henry Fenwick, 'The Production', *The BBC TV Shakespeare: Henry VI Part One* (London: BBC 1983), pp. 22–3.

26 Henry Fenwick, 'Dialogues of Disintegration', *Radio Times* (1 January 1983).

27 *The BBC TV Shakespeare: Henry VI, Part Two* (London: BBC 1983), p. 20.

28 Stanley Wells, 'The History of the Whole Contention', *Times Higher Educational Supplement* (4 February 1983), p. 105.

29 See Holderness, *Shakespeare's History*, Introduction 3, 'Drama and Society'.

30 Michael Billington, 'Why old Bill needs rejuvenating', *The Guardian* (30 December 1982).

31 See Michael Bogdanov interviewed in Graham Holderness, ed., *The Shakespeare Myth* (Manchester: Manchester University Press, 1988), Chapter 8.

32 See Bogdanov, *op. cit.*, and Jonathan Miller interviewed in Holderness, *Shakespeare Myth*, Chapter 18. See also Hallinan, 'Jonathan Miller on *The Shakespeare Plays*', p.140.

33 See the three booklets produced to accompany the series, which compare interestingly in style and approach to the two-volume publication which accompanied the BBC Time-Life series – Michael Bogdanov and Joss Buckley, *Shakespeare Lives!* (London: Channel 4/Quintet Films, 1983); and Roger Sales (ed.) *Shakespeare in Perspective* (London: BBC/Ariel Books, 2 vols, 1982 and 1985).

34 Christopher J. McCullough, 'The Cambridge Connection' in Holderness, *Shakespeare Myth*, pp. 112–121.

35 Trevor Nunn, 'Foreword' to John Barton, *Playing Shakespeare*
    (London: Methuen 1984).
36 The Peacock committee reported in 1986 on the financing of the
    BBC. Contrary to Tory government expectations, the committee
    did not recommend the introduction of advertising; but its propos-
    als recommended the eventual replacement of the licence fee by
    direct subscription.
37 Noel Annan, 'A programme for the future?', *Times Literary Supple-
    ment* (12 September 1986), p. 993: 'Being employed by the BBC
    should mean that you accept obligations that do not affect other
    broadcasters ... as a national institution ... the BBC owes duties to
    the state'.
39 *Report of the Committee on the Future of Broadcasting* (London:
    HMSO, 1977), p. 325.

Two: Shakespeare Rescheduled (1998)

First published as 'Shakespeare Rescheduled' (with Carol Banks), in
Boxed Sets: Television Representations of Shakespeare, edited by
Jeremy Ridgman (The Arts Council and John Libbey, 1998), pp.
173–185.

1 Our preference is to use original titles, but for the reader's conven-
   ience we have here employed those in more general use.
2 See for example Leah Marcus, *Puzzling Shakespeare: Local Reading
   and its Discontents* (Berkeley: University of Berkeley Press, 1988);
   and Gary Taylor, *Reinventing Shakespeare: A Cultural History
   1642-1986* (London: Weidenfeld and Nicholson, 1989).
3 Stanley Wells and Gary Taylor, editors of *The Oxford Shakespeare:
   William Shakespeare the Complete Works* (Oxford: Oxford University
   Press, 1988), return the plays to their presumed order of composition. This is the edition used for quotations from Shakespeare in
   this article.
4 Tillyard, *Shakespeare's History Plays* (London: Chatto and Windus,
   1944, 1960 edn.), pp. 234 and 147.
5 Notably Lily B. Campbell, *Shakespeare's Histories: Mirrors of
   Elizabethan Policy* (San Marino, CA: Huntingdon Library, 1947);
   G. Wilson Knight, *The Olive and the Sword* (Oxford: Oxford
   University Press, 1944); and J. Dover Wilson and T.C. Worsley,

Shakespeare's Histories at Stratford 1951 (London: Max Reinhardt, 1952).

6   Richard David, 'Shakespeare's History Plays: Epic or Drama?', *Shakespeare Survey*, 6 (1953), p.129.

7   Wilson and Worsley, *Shakespeare's Histories at Stratford*, pp. xviii–xix

8   David, 'Shakespeare's History Plays', p.129.

9   Cedric Messina, 'Preface' to *The BBC TV Shakespeare: Richard II* (London: BBC Publications, 1978), p. 8.

10   J. F. Andrews, 'Cedric Messina Discusses *The Shakespeare Plays*', *Shakespeare Quarterly* 30:2 (1979), p.137.

11   These films discussed in Chapter Three.

12   See Seymour Chatman, *Story and Discourse: Narrative Structure in Fiction and Film* (Ithaca: Cornell University Press,1978), pp. 28–31.

13   Tillyard, *Shakespeare's Histories*, and Jan Kott, *Shakespeare Our Contemporary*, translated by Boleslaw Taborski (London: Methuen, 1967).

14   Alan Sinfield in Dollimore and Sinfield (eds), *Political Shakespeare* (Manchester: Manchester University Press,1985), p. 131.

15   Hall quoted by Sinfield in *Political Shakespeare*, pp. 160 and 162.

16   Kott, *Shakespeare Our Contemporary*, p. 25.

17   *Political Shakespeare*, p. 162.

18   Kott, *Shakespeare Our Contemporary*, p. 39.

19   On oral structures see Walter Ong, *Orality and Literacy: The Technologizing of the Word* (London: Routledge,1988).

20   Wilson and Worsley, *The Histories at Stratford*, p. 22.

21   *The Cronicle History of Henry the Fift* (Q1, 1600), edited by Graham Holderness and Bryan Loughrey (Hemel Hempstead: Harvester Wheatsheaf, 1993), p. 60.

22   See Anne Barton, 'The king disguised: Shakespeare's *Henry V* and the comic history' in Joseph G. Price (ed.) *The Triple Bond* (Philadelphia: Pennsylvania State University Press, 1975).

23   Holderness and Loughrey, *Cronicle Historie*, p. 73.

24   See Wells and Taylor *The Oxford Shakespeare* (1988), p. 483

25   Murray Roston, *Renaissance Perspectives in Literature and the Visual Arts* (Princeton: Princeton University Press, 1987), p. 203.

26   Charles Avery, *Florentine Renaissance Sculpture* (London: John Murray, 1970), pp. 51–2.

27 The comparison between diptychs and the two parts of *Henry IV* also made by Sherman H. Hawkins, '*Henry IV*: The Structural Problem Revisited', *Shakespeare Quarterly* 33:3 (1982), pp. 134–45.

28 See Michael Baxandall, *Painting and Experience in Fifteenth Century Italy* (Oxford: Oxford University Press, 2nd edn. 1988), pp. 94–108.

29 Perry Brooks, *Piero della Francesca: The Arezzo Frescoes*, (New York: Rizzoli International Publishing,1992), unpaginated.

30 Tim Hallinan, 'Jonathan Miller on *The Shakespeare Plays*', *Shakespeare Quarterly* 32 (1981), p. 134.

31 Milton Crane, 'Shakespeare on Television', *Shakespeare Quarterly* 112 (1961), p. 326.

32 Leon Battista Alberti, *On Painting* (1435–6), trans. John R. Spencer (New Haven and London: Yale University Press, 2nd edn., 1996), p. 77.

33 BBC's Royal Charter and IBA Act, as quoted in Raymond Kuhn, *The Politics of Broadcasting* (London: Croom Helm, 1985), p. 15.

34 Kuhn, *Politics of Broadcasting*, p. 36

35 Hallinan, 'Jonathan Miller on *The Shakespeare Plays*', p. 145.

36 Raymond Williams, *Television: Technology and Technological Form* (London: Fontana, 1974), pp. 88–90.

37 J. C. Bulman and H. R. Coursen, *Shakespeare on Television* (Hanover, NH: University Presses of New England, 1988), pp. 209–10.

38 James Joyce, *A Portrait of the Artist as a Young Man* (Harmondsworth: Penguin, 1960), p. 215.

Three: Shakespeare and Cinema (1985, 1991)

The first part of this chapter was originally published as 'Radical Potentiality and Institutional Closure: Shakespeare in Film and Television', in *Political Shakespeare*, edited by Jonathan Dollimore and Alan Sinfield (Manchester: MUP, 1985), pp. 182–201. The second part as '*A Midsummer Night's Dream*: Film and Fantasy', in *Critical Essays on A Midsummer Night's Dream*, edited by Bryan Loughrey and Linda Cookson (Harlow: Longman, 1991), pp. 63–71.

1   For which see, for instance, Roger Manvell, *Shakespeare and the Film* (New York: Praeger, 1971, South Brunswick, N.J.: A.S. Barnes,

revised 1979), and Jack Jorgens: *Shakespeare on Film* (Bloomington: Indiana University Press, 1977).

2   Joint Matriculation Board *Examiners' Reports*, Vol 1 *Arts and Social Sciences* (1974), p. 9.

3   Catherine Belsey, 'Shakespeare and Film', *Literature/Film Quarterly*, XI:2 (Spring 1983).

4   S.D. Lawder, 'Film: Art of the Twentieth Century', *Yale Alumni Magazine* (May 1968), p. 33.

5   See David Robinson, *Financial Times* (23 July 1971), quoted by Jorgens, *Shakespeare on Film*, p. 244.

6   Max Reinhardt, Foreword to *A Midsummer Night's Dream* (New York: Grosset and Dunlap, 1935), p. v.

7   Peter Brook, 'Shakespeare on Three Screens', *Sight and Sound*, 34 (1965), p. 68; Grigori Kozintsev, *Shakespeare, Time and Conscience* (New York: Hill and Wang, 1966), p. 29; Frank Kermode, 'Shakespeare in the Movies', *New York Review of Books* (10 October 1972); J. Blumenthal, '*Macbeth* into Throne of Blood', *Sight and Sound*, 34 (1965), p. 191.

8   The film has been very usefully discussed in this latter context by Ana Laura Zambrano, '*Throne of Blood*: Kurosawa's *Macbeth*', *Literature Film Quarterly*, II:3 (Summer 1974).

9   Donald Richie, *The Films of Akira Kurosawa*, (Berkeley and Los Angeles: University of California Press, 1965), p. 117.

10 John Gerlach, 'Shakespeare, Kurosawa and *Macbeth*', *Literature/Film Quarterly* I:4 (Fall 1973), p. 352.

Four: Shakespeare Rewound (1993)

First published as 'Shakespeare Rewound', *Shakespeare Survey*, 45 (1993), pp. 63–74.

1   The productions to be discussed are:
Hamlet (1979), produced and directed by Celestino Coronado. A Royal College of Art production, in association with the Design Department of North London Polytechnic. Hamlet, the Ghost and Laertes, Anthony and David Meyer; Ophelia and Gertrude, Helen Mirren; Claudius, Barry Stanton; Polonius, Quentin Crisp.
Hamlet (1987), adapted and directed for the stage by Roland Kenyon with Cambridge Experimental Theatre. Video production

by Cambridgeshire College of Arts and Technology Audio-Visual Unit. Directed by Rod MacDonald. Edited by Richard Spaul and Rod Macdonald. *Gertrude*, Melanie Revill; *Claudius*, Richard Spaul; *Ophelia*, Tricia Hitchcock; *Polonius*, Alan Wilson.

The Tempest (1980), directed by Derek Jarman. Produced by Guy Ford and Mordecai Schreiber. Edited by Richard Melling. Designed by Yolande Sonnabend. *Prospero*, Heathcote Williams; *Miranda*, Toyah Wilcox; *Ferdinand*, David Meyer; *Caliban*, Jack Birkett ('the Incredible Orlando'); *Ariel*, Karl Johnson.

2   Roger Manvell, *Shakespeare and the Film* (New York: Praeger, 1971, South Brunswick, N.J.: A. S. Barnes, revised, 1979); Charles Eckert (ed.), *Focus on Shakespearean Films* (New Jersey: Prentice Hall, 1972); Jack Jorgens, *Shakespeare on Film* (Bloomington: Indiana University Press, 1977).

3   See Manvell, *Shakespeare and the Film*, p. 21: 'It was better to wait until Shakespeare's plays could be filmed with speech'; and Jorgens, *Shakespeare on Film*, who speaks of 'one-and two-reelers struggling to render great poetic drama in dumb show' (p. 1). Robert Hamilton Ball's *Shakespeare on Silent Film: A Strange Eventful History* (London: George, Allen and Unwin, 1968) of course covers the silent era, though it is (remarkably) by no means free from the assumption that Shakespeare without the spoken word is not truly 'Shakespeare'.

4   Anthony Davies, *Filming Shakespeare's Plays* (Cambridge: Cambridge University Press, 1988), p. 152.

5   But see John Collick's review of Davies in *Critical Survey*, 2:1 (1990), pp. 108–11.

6   John Collick, *Shakespeare, Cinema and Society* (Manchester: Manchester University Press, 1989).

7   Antonin Artaud, *The Theatre and its Double* (1964), trans. Victor Corti (London: Calder and Boyers, 1970).

8   Charles Marowitz, *The Marowitz Shakespeare* (London: Calder and Boyars, 1978).

9   Laurence Senelick, *Gordon Craig's Moscow Hamlet: a reconstruction* (Westport, Conn. and London: Greenwood Press, 1982), p. 68.

10 Gaston Melies, quoted in Ball, *Shakespeare on Silent Film*, p. 34.

11 *Hamlet: A Guide*, Cambridge Experimental Theatre, Cambridgeshire College of Arts and Technology Audio-Visual Unit (1987), p. 7.

12   David L. Hirst, *Text and Performance: The Tempest* (London: Macmillan, 1984), pp. 54–5.

13   Peter Brook, *The Empty Space* (1968) (Harmondsworth: Penguin, 1972), pp. 96–8.

Five: Henry V (1984)

First published as 'Agincourt 1944: Readings on the Shakespeare Myth', *Literature and History*, 10:1 (1984), pp. 24–45.

1   The application of these principles to Shakespeare is the subject of the companion volume *Cultural Shakespeare: essays in the Shakespeare Myth* (Hatfield: University of Hertfordshire Press, 2001).

2   See *Times Higher Educational Supplement* (11 February 1983), p. 12.

3   Tony Bennett, 'Text and History', in Peter Widdowson (ed.), *Re-Reading English* (1982), pp. 224–5.

4   Peter Widdowson, 'Hardy in History', *Literature and History*, Vol 9:1 (Spring 1983).

5   G. Wilson Knight, *The Olive and the Sword* (Oxford: Oxford University Press, 1944). For details of the production of *This Sceptred Isle*, see G. Wilson Knight, *Shakespearean Production* (London: Faber and Faber, 1964).

6   E. M. W. Tillyard, *Shakespeare's History Plays* (London: Chatto and Windus, 1944).

7   See, e.g. L.C. Knights, 'Shakespeare and Profit Inflations', *Scrutiny*, Vol V, No. 1 (June 1936).

8   See 'Cato', *Guilty Men* (London: Gollancz, 1940), p. 63.

9   Angus Calder, *The People's War* (London: Jonathan Cape, 1969), quotation from p. 17.

10   Henry Pelling, *Britain and the Second World War* (London: Collins, 1970).

11   C. Woolf and J. Moorcroft Wilson, *Authors take Sides on the Falklands* (London: Woolf, 1982), as quoted in Terence Hawkes, *That Shakespeherian Rag* (London: Methuen, 1986), p.68.

12   Clayton C. Hutton, *The Making of Henry V* (London: The Author, printed by Ernest J. Day & Co., 1944).

13   See, e.g. Frederick Aiken, 'Shakespeare on the Screen', *Screen Education* (Sept-Oct 1963), p. 33: '*Henry V* was the one with William

Walton's music and the charge of the knights at Agincourt – magnificent stuff, if not exactly Shakespeare'; and J. Blumenthal, 'Macbeth' into Throne of Blood', Sight and Sound, Vol 34 (1965), p. 194; ' … Olivier's desperate attempt at the end of Henry V to add a dash of "cinema" in the form of an equine extravaganza'.

14 Henry V, Chorus, Act 1, 8–14. All quotations from the Arden Shakespeare edition, J.H. Walter (ed.) (1954).

15 R.S. Wallace and Alma Hansen (eds), Holinshed's Chronicles, Richard II 1398–1400, and Henry V (Oxford: Clarendon Press, 1917), p. 78.

16 See William Hazlitt, Characters of Shakespeare's Plays [1817] (Cambridge: Cambridge University Press, 1908).

17 See also Michael Balcon (et. al.), Twenty Years of British Film (1925–45) (London: Falcon Press, 1947).

18 David M. Bergeron, Shakespeare: A Study and Research Guide (New York: St. Martins Press, 1975), p. 56.

19 Derek Traversi, Shakespeare from Richard II to Henry V (London: Hollis and Carter, 1958).

20 John Wilders, The Lost Garden (London: Macmillan, 1978).

Six: The Taming of the Shrew (1989)

First published as 'Franco Zeffirelli (1966)', in Graham Holderness, Shakespeare in Performance: The Taming of the Shrew (Manchester: MUP, 1989), pp. 49–72.

1 Catherine Belsey, 'Shakespeare and film', Literature/Film Quarterly, XI:2 (Spring 1983).

2 Andre Bazin, 'Theatre and cinema', in What is Cinema? Vol. 1 (1967), p. 106.

3 Carey Harrison, Sight and Sound, 36 (Spring 1967), p. 98.

4 Zeffirelli in a programme note for the Old Vic Romeo and Juliet, 1960; quoted in Jill L. Levenson, Shakespeare in Performance: Romeo and Juliet (Manchester: Manchester University Press, 1987), p. 85.

5 John Francis Lane, Films and Filming (October 1966), p. 50.

6 Richard Roud in the Guardian (3 March 1967).

7 Jack J. Jorgens, Shakespeare on Film (Bloomington: Indiana University Press, 1979), p. 71.

8   See especially Mikhail Bakhtin, *Rabelais and his World*, trans. Helen Iswolsky (Cambridge, Mass: CIT Press, 1968).

9   See Graham Holderness, *Shakespeare's History* (Dublin: Gill and Macmillan, 1985), pp. 79–87.

10 Quoted in A.P. Rossiter, *English Drama from Early Times to the Elizabethans* (New York: Barnes and Noble, 1967), pp. 64–5.

11 For further discussion of 'carnival' see C.L. Barber, *Shakespeare's Festive Comedy* (Princeton: Princeton University Press, 1959); Michael D. Bristol, *Carnival and Theatre,* (London: Methuen, 1985).

12 Roger Manvell, *Shakespeare and the Film* (New York: Praeger, 1971, South Brunswick, N.J.: A.S. Barnes, revised, 1979), describes the various locations used: p. 100.

13 Penelope Gilliatt, *Observer* (5 March 1967).

14 Patrick Gibbs, *Daily Telegraph* (28 February 1967).

15 Stephen Farber, *Film Quarterly*, XX:1 (Fall 1967), p. 61.

16 Tori Haring-Smith, *From Farce to Metadrama: a stage history of 'The Taming of the Shrew'*, *1594–1983*, (Westport, Conn. and London: Greenwood Press, 1985).

17 Alexander Walker, *Evening Standard* (2 March 1967).

18 David Robinson, *Financial Times* (3 March 1967).

19 Penelope Houston, *Spectator* (10 March 1967).

20 Felix Barker, *Evening News* (2 March 1967).

21 *Monthly Film Bulletin*, XXXIV: 399 (April 1967), p. 58.

22 *Evening Standard* (5 July 1965).

23 *The Sun* (28 February 1967).

24 *Playboy* (June 1967).

25 Robert Robinson, *Sunday Telegraph* (5 March 1967).

26 Dilys Powell, *Sunday Times* (5 March 1967).

27 Ian Christie, *Daily Mail* (28 February 1967).

28 Gerald Kaufman, *Listener* (9 March 1967).

29 *Morning Star* (4 March 1967).

30 *New Statesman* (3 March 1967).

Seven: Romeo and Juliet (1991)

First published as 'Romeo and Juliet: Myth and Universality', *Literatura, Historia e Mito* (Belo Horizonte, 1991), pp. 29–38.

1   The Leonard Bernstein and Stephen Sondheim stage musical *West*

Side Story was premiered at The Winter Garden Theatre, New York in September 1957 (directed and choreographed by Jerome Robbins); it came to London in December of the following year, and the film version (Robert Wise Productions), was released in October 1961, distributed by United Artists. The film attracted big audiences and won many prizes.

2   Joan Lingard, *Across the Barricades* (London: Hamish Hamilton, 1977).

3   Michael Bogdanov's 1986 RSC production of *Romeo and Juliet* was reviewed by Nicholas Shrimpton in *Shakespeare Survey* 40 (1988), pp. 178–80.

4   The text of Arthur Brooke's *The Tragicall Historye of Romeus and Iuliet, written first in Italian by Bandell, and nowe in Englishe by Ar.Br.* (1562) is reprinted in Geoffrey Bullough, ed., *Narrative and Dramatic Sources of Shakespeare* Vol. 1 (London: Routledge and Kegan Paul, 1957), and extracts are included in the Appendices to the New Cambridge edition of *Romeo and Juliet*, edited by G. Blakemore Evans (Cambridge: Cambridge University Press, 1984), and the Arden edition, edited by Brian Gibbons (London: Routledge, 1988).

5   Auden's view from the commentary to *Romeo and Juliet* in *The Laurel Shakespeare* series (1958), general editor Francis Fergusson, pp. 21–39, as noted by G. Blakemore Evans in his 'Introduction' to the New Cambridge edition (1984), p. 14.

6   *Mr. William Shakespeare his Comedies Histories and Tragedies*, edited by Edmund Capell in 10 vols (London: J & R Thonson, 1768).

7   Stage direction for Q2–4. Modern editors often follow Theobald (1733) by adding the stage direction 'Exeunt' to clear the stage before the servingmen enter. See, for example, Peter Alexander's edition, *William Shakespeare: The Complete Works* (London: Collins, 1951), and Wells and Taylor (eds), *William Shakespeare: The Complete Works* (Oxford: Clarendon Press, 1988).

8   Scene locations as in the Rowe edition of 1709; similar descriptions are repeated Theobald (1733) and in Garrick's Theatre Royal edition (Dublin: W. Brien and R. Jones, 1747), and continue through Edward Bowden's first Arden edition (London: Methuen, 1900), to J. Dover Wilson's (assisted by George Ian Duthie) edition for the Cambridge New Shakespeare Series (Cambridge University Press,

1955), finally to be relocated to the notes by G. Blakemore Evans in the New Cambridge Edition of 1984.

9   In Rowe the scene change at Act IV, scene iv, is identified as follows 'Scene changes to Capulet's Hall', and at Act IV, scene v: 'Scene changes to Juliet's Chamber. Juliet on a bed'. As Andrew Gurr points out, in Elizabethan and Jacobean theatres the scene was changed simply by one person departing and another entering, but later the word 'scene' itself came to mean the canvas flats of scenery (wing-and-shutter scenes) which provided backgrounds for different localities. See Gurr, *The Shakespearean Stage 1574–1642*, (Cambridge: Cambridge University Press, 1970), p. 117.

10   Theobald, 1733.

11   See engraving of Garrick's tomb scene by R. S. Ravenet (1753), reproduced in the 'Introduction' to the New Cambridge edition (1984), p. 35, plate 3.

12   In the latter part of the nineteenth century attempts to create a sense of historical accuracy resulted in scenery which reproduced actual locations in Verona (the Piazza dell' Erbe and the Piazza Dante) and interiors copied from early paintings.

13   See artist's impression of the last scene in Irving's production at the Lyceum, London in 1882, in the New Cambridge edition (1984), p. 42, plate 7.

14   Jack J. Jorgens, 'Franco Zeffirelli's *Romeo and Juliet*', *Shakespeare on Film* (Bloomington and London: Indiana University Press, 1977), pp. 79–91.

Bibliography

૪૦

Ball, Robert Hamilton. *Shakespeare on Silent Film: A Strange Eventful History* (London: Allen & Unwin, and New York: Theater Arts Books, 1968).

Boose, Lynda E. and Richard Burt, eds. *Shakespeare, The Movie: Popularizing the Plays on Film, TV, and Video* (London and New York: Routledge, 1997).

Buchman, Lorne Michael. *Still in Movement: Shakespeare on Screen* (Oxford and New York: Oxford University Press, 1991).

Bulman, J.C. and H.R. Coursen, eds. *Shakespeare on Television: An Anthology of Essays and Reviews* (Hanover: University Press of New England, 1988).

Burnett, Mark Thornton, ed. *Shakespeare, Film, Fin-de-Siecle* (London: Macmillan, 2000).

Cartmell, Deborah. *Interpreting Shakespeare on Screen* (London: Macmillan, 2000).

Chedgzoy, Kate. *Shakespeare's Queer Children: Sexual Politics and Contemporary Culture* (Manchester: Manchester University Press, and New York: St. Martins Press, 1995).

Collick, John. *Shakespeare, Cinema, and Society* (Manchester: Manchester University Press, and New York: St. Martin's Press, 1989).

Coursen, Herbert R. *Shakespeare in production: whose history?* (Athens: Ohio University Press, 1996).

Coursen, Herbert R. *Shakespeare: the two traditions* (Madison, NJ: Fairleigh Dickinson University Press, 1999).

Coursen, Herbert R. *Teaching Shakespeare with film and television: a guide* (Westport, Conn.: Greenwood Press, 1997).

Coursen, Herbert R. *Watching Shakespeare on Television* (Rutherford, NJ: Fairleigh Dickinson University Press; London; Cranbury, NJ: Associated University Presses, 1993).

Davies, Anthony. *Filming Shakespeare's Plays: The Adaptations of Laurence Olivier, Orson Welles, Peter Brook, and Akira Kurosawa* (Cambridge and New York: Cambridge University Press, 1988).

Davies, Anthony and Stanley Wells. *Shakespeare and the Moving Image: The Plays on Film and Television* (Cambridge and New York: Cambridge University Press, 1994).

Donaldson, Peter Samuel. *Shakespearean Films/Shakespearean Directors* (Boston: Unwin Hyman, 1990).

Eckert, Charles W. ed. *Focus on Shakespearean Films* (Englewood Cliffs, N.J., Prentice-Hall, 1972).

Hodgdon, Barbara. *The Shakespeare Trade: performances and appropriations* (Philadelphia: University of Pennsylvania Press, 1999).

Jorgens, Jack J. *Shakespeare on Film* (Bloomington: Indiana University Press, 1977).

Manvell, Roger. *Shakespeare and the Film* (New York: Praeger, 1971; revised and updated South Brunswick, NJ: A.S. Barnes, 1979).

MacCabe, Colin and Olivia Stewart, eds. *The BBC and Public Service Broadcasting* (Manchester: Manchester University Press, 1986).

McGuire, Philip C. *Speechless Dialect: Shakespeare's Open Silences* (Berkeley: University of California Press, 1985).

Morris, Peter. *Shakespeare on Film* (Ottawa: Canadian Film Institute, 1972).

Pilkington, Ace G. *Screening Shakespeare from Richard II to Henry V* (Newark: University of Delaware Press; London and Cranbury, NJ: Associated University Presses, 1991).

Rothwell, Kenneth S. *A History of Shakespeare on Screen: A Century of Film and Television* (Cambridge and New York: Cambridge University Press, 1999).

Rothwell, Kenneth S. and Annabelle Henkin Melzer. *Shakespeare on Screen: An International Filmography and Videography* (New York: Neal-Schuman, 1990).

Shaughnessy, Robert, ed. *Shakespeare on Film* (London and New York: St. Martin's Press, 1998).